THEODORE ROETHKE'S MEDITATIVE SEQUENCES

CONTEMPLATION

AND THE

CREATIVE PROCESS

by

Ann T. Foster

Studies in Art and Religious Interpretation
Volume Four

The Edwin Mellen Press
Lewiston/Queenston

Library of Congress Cataloging in Publication Data

Foster, Ann T.
  Theodore Roethke's meditative sequences.

  (Studies in art and religious interpretation ; v. 4)
  Bibliography: p.
  Includes index.
  1. Roethke, Theodore, 1908-1963--Religion and ethics.
2. Meditation in literature. 3. Contemplation in
literature. 4. Mysticism in literature. 5. Creation
(Literary, artistic, etc.) I. Title. II. Series.
PS3535.039Z63 1985   811'.54   85-3041
ISBN 0-88946-555-X

Studies in Art and Religious Interpretation
Series ISBN 0-88946-956-3

The Edwin Mellen Press   The Edwin Mellen Press
Box 450   Box 67
Lewiston, New York   Queenston, Ontario
USA 14092   Canada L0S 1L0

Printed in the United States of America

for my mother,
whose friendship and encouragement have made this
  possible

ACKNOWLEDGEMENTS

Acknowledgement is gratefully made to Beatrice Roethke Lushington for her permission to quote from unpublished materials at the University of Washington Library.

Poetic excerpts from the book *The Collected Poems of Theodore Roethke*, Copyright © 1957, 1958, 1959, 1960, 1961, 1962, 1963 by Beatrice Roethke as Administratrix of the Estate of Theodore Roethke; Copyright © 1946, 1947, 1948, 1949, 1950, 1951, 1952, 1955, 1956, 1957, 1958, 1961 by Theodore Roethke are reprinted by permission of Doubleday & Company, Inc.

TABLE OF CONTENTS

PREFACE

This book hopes to demonstrate the meditative process by which Roethke creates "A poetry of longing: not for escape, but a greater reality" (Roethke Notebooks, Reel 9 #123).* The primary aim of the study is to analyze the meditative structure in Roethke's major sequences and to examine the mental processes employed by the speakers. Using the powers of the soul--memory, understanding and will--and a meditative process involving composition, analysis and colloquy, Roethke strives to create a self with spiritual identity and to reach toward that Unity which is the ground of the universe.

Most scholars--and I am no exception--find that their projects evolve gradually, the original idea being only one element of the final topic. I began by exploring the mystical aspects of Roethke's poetry, particularly his use of the Mystic Way. Karl Malkoff, Richard Blessing and Rosemary Sullivan had mentioned some of Roethke's reading in mystical literature, principally Evelyn Underhill's Mysticism, and had quoted significant references to mystical thought from Roethke's Notebooks. I was also guided by William Heyen's article "The Divine Abyss: Theodore Roethke's Mysticism." Despite the fact that I did not agree totally with his analysis of the Mystic Way in Roethke's poem "The Abyss," his reading of the poem prompted me to turn to Roethke's unpublished papers for additional evidence of the poet's study of mysticism. I was eager to learn if Roethke had read other major works in the field and, ultimately, I wanted to deal with the question of Roethke as poet-mystic.

I spent two years reading Roethke's Notebooks in relation to the poetry and examining the books in Roethke's private library, particularly those in religion and philosophy. This close study has

convinced me that the quest of the mystic is instilled
in the poetry because for Roethke the poetic process is
the form of meditation by which he seeks to reshape the
self and journey toward union with Absolute Reality.
This basic premise has led me to consider Roethke's use
of contemplation in the creative act and to analyze the
sequences within the meditative tradition. In addition
to Underhill's Mysticism, I have drawn heavily on
Roethke's Notebooks in the study as well as several
works from his library, including St. Francis de Sales'
Introduction to the Devout Life. I am indebted to
Arnold Stein in his Introduction to Theodore Roethke:
Essays on the Poetry for stating the connection between
contemplation and Roethke's mode of composition.
Expanding on this idea, I have attempted to explore the
manner in which poetry and meditation meet in the
creative act. The sequences are then analyzed
according to the meditative principles rooted in the
poetry. As a corollary of this study, I have discussed
the Degrees of Interior Prayer revealed in the poetry
to determine whether the search for the inner self is
completed and the mystic consciousness realized.

Two discussions of Roethke's mysticism have been
published in recent years, but none has dealt with the
meditative elements in the sequences. Jay Parini, in
Theodore Roethke: An American Romantic, analyzes
Roethke's quest for illumination in the posthumous
volume, The Far Field, noting the meditative genre in
passing. In his conclusion Parini refers to Roethke as
a meditative poet, but since this has not been his
primary concern, he has only mentioned briefly the
discipline's use of memory and colloquy, a conversation
with God. Neal Bowers presents a systematic study of
the Mystic Way in the poetry in Theodore Roethke: The

Journey from I to Otherwise. He points out the
importance of meditation to Roethke's own mystical
strivings, but he equates this method with
contemplation and he does not analyze the meditative
discipline imbedded in the poetry. Although Neal
Bowers and I agree that mysticism informs Roethke's
poetry, our central purposes are different. He focuses
as much on Roethke's life as the poetry, considering
the relationship between the poet's manic-depressive
syndrome and the Mystic Way followed in the poetry.
The intent of this study, on the other hand, is to
treat Roethke as a poet in the meditative tradition
whose poetry is infused with mystical thought. It is
my hope that this analysis of the structure and themes
of Roethke's meditative sequences will complement and
go beyond the existing Roethke criticism.

Several individuals have been generous to assist
me in completing this project. I am especially
grateful to Harry Morris and Lawrence Cunningham of
Florida State University for their guidance and
critical judgment. Their encourgement is sincerely
appreciated. I would also like to acknowledge Herbert
Richardson of The Edwin Mellen Press for his valuable
assistance. Brief portions of this book have appeared
in the article "Theodore Roethke as Meditative Poet:
An Analysis of 'Meditations of an Old Woman,'" published in Studies in the Literary Imagination.

I

INTRODUCTION

"Affinities: between love of poetic
form and the religious spirit."
            --Roethke Notebooks (3 #30)

"I am a religious poet. Why? Because
of self-knowledge."
            --Roethke Notebooks (4 #46)

"Poetry: essential action outward."
            --Roethke Notebooks (8 #115)

Theodore Roethke is a poet for whom the creative process is a religious activity. In the notebooks he expresses an affinity between the love of poetic form and the religious spirit because their common source is found in the deep recesses of the soul. The creative spirit which engenders poetry resides in the seat of the soul where the inner self is hidden and where the germ of religious ideas exists. For Roethke, then, "Poetic and religious are identical states of mind" (11 #152). Their mental attitudes and fundamental impulses are the same. Both endeavors are animated by intuition through a form of concentration, whether meditation or contemplation, and both seek to grasp inner and outer reality, the reality of the self, the world, or even God.

The poet must be alert and receptive to the poetic intuition which, as Jacques Maritain says in Creative Intuition in Art and Poetry, is born in "the spiritual unconscious, or rather, preconscious," emerges into consciousness, and is then directed at once toward the inner reality or "subjectivity of the poet" and the infinite reality of all things of the world.[1] As we shall see, the spiritual journey revealed in Roethke's poetry incorporates this twofold movement. It is at

once an interior journey in which the protagonist
achieves self-identity and an outward quest in which
the self is transcended and the inner reality of the
world is apprehended. Thus Roethke not only practices
but demonstrates in the poetry the processes which
Maritain asserts are inseparable requirements of poetic
creation: knowledge of the self and "of the objective
reality of the outer and inner world. . . through
affective union."[2] This poetic knowledge is united in
the depths of our being, Maritain states, abiding
naturally in ourselves by inclination. It is no
wonder, then, that Maritain is convinced that "poetic
intuition and poetic knowledge are both one of the
basic manifestations of man's spiritual nature."[3] This
study is based on the belief that Roethke's creative
mode and the movement of the poetry itself are
embodiments of this idea.

The effort of returning to the inner self and
utilizing its insights is a necessary activity of
poetic creativity and the religious life. As the
creative self is the real personhood of the artist, not
the ego, so the self involved in the spiritual journey
is the "inner I," not the restricted, self-centered
"I." This creative self is the true self which is
engaged by the work of poetry and religion in the
center of the soul. In Prayer and Poetry, Henri
Bremond analyzes the twofold nature of the human
personality--"the distinction between the two selves":

> Animus, the surface self; Anima, the deep
> self; Animus, rational knowledge; the Anima,
> mystical or poetic knowledge. . . . The I,
> who feeds on notions and words, and enchants
> himself by doing so; the Me, who is united to
> realities; the Me, who receives the visits of

God; the I, who often delays them, obstructs
them, volatilises them in words, and thus
loses the benefit of them.[4]

Roethke echoes Bremond's contrast in the
notebooks, though the terminology is reversed: "The
empirical self (the me) and the knowing self (I)" (15
#210). It is the knowing self that resides at the apex
of the soul. The existence of the two selves is
further implied by Roethke in his essay, "On
'Identity,'" when he characterizes the effort to "break
from self-involvement, from I to Otherwise, or maybe
even to Thee" as being "accompanied by a loss of the
'I,' the purely human ego, to another center."[5] The
center Roethke refers to is the deeper self, man's
spiritual faculty. Like Bremond, Evelyn Underhill
thinks of this transcendental faculty as the essential
element of mystical psychological life. In _Mysticism_,
she describes it as the "hidden self":

> a self which the circumstances of diurnal
> life usually keep "below the threshold" of
> his consciousness, and which thus becomes one
> of the factors of his "subliminal life."
> This hidden self is the primary agent of
> mysticism, and lives a "substantial" life in
> touch with the real or transcendental world.[6]

Thus the inner self is the creative source of poetry
and the primary agent of mysticism. The task of both
arts is to reach this hidden self and to bring it forth
into consciousness in order that its intuitions may be
known and felt. Clearly, we have now raised the
question of the relationship between poetry and
mysticism, the poet and the mystic, issues which will
be considered later in this introduction as well as in
the final chapter.

When the poet touches the center of the soul, he not only receives the aid of creative intuition but also the other agents or powers of the soul. Since the poem is the fruit of the totality of the poet's being, he must bend toward and be open to the workings of all the spiritual elements at the core of the self. Jacques Maritain has illustrated the interplay of these powers:

> . . . there is in this spiritual unconscious a root activity in which the intellect and the imagination, as well as the powers of desire, love, and emotion, are engaged in common. The powers of the soul envelop one another, the universe of sense perception is in the universe of imagination, which is in the universe of intelligence. And they are all, within the intellect, stirred and activated by the light of the Illuminating Intellect.[7]

When one examines the dynamic motion described by Maritain, it becomes evident that, for him, the "imagination proceeds or flows from the essence of the soul through the intellect, and that the external senses proceed from the essence of the soul through imagination."[8] For our purposes the important aspect of Maritain's diagram of interpenetrating cones is the circle lowest in the soul, representing "the intuitive data afforded by external Sensation"; this sensation, which is "almost unconscious," emanates from the depths of the soul and "becomes sense perception when it is interpreted and structured through the instrumentality of memory, imagination, and the other 'internal senses'"; it then radiates upward to aid the activity of the external senses, thereafter moving through the imagination to the intellect.[9]

This interaction must be stressed, for Roethke believes that the poet is "the intuitive man":

"We think by feeling. What is there to know?" This, in its essence, is a description of the metaphysical poet who thinks with his body: an idea for him can be real as the smell of a flower or a blow on the head. And those so lucky as to bring their whole sensory equipment to bear on the process of thought grow faster, jump more frequently from one plateau to another more often (SP 19, 27).

To think by feeling means to focus on the life of the external senses, allowing memory, imagination, and the other internal senses to interpret the intuitive data received from the external world. When this process is combined with what Roethke calls "intensity in the seeing"--a form of contemplation--the poet may "jump more frequently from one plateau to another," experiencing "a heightened consciousness" (SP 25). Roethke comments on this process in "On Identity,'" a movement which is initiated by perceiving the essence of another being:

It is paradoxical that a very sharp sense of the identity of some other being--and in some instances, even an inanimate thing--brings a corresponding heightening and awareness of one's own self, and, even more mysteriously, in some instances, a feeling of the oneness of the universe (SP 25).

If the internal and external senses are brought to bear on the intellect through the imagination, the poet may

reach "the first stage in mystical illumination": "The
sense that all is one and one is all" (SP 26). Through
creative intuition, then, the poet touches the inner
life of the soul--the spiritual self--and may even
reach a higher level of consciousness. By means of ths
intuitive state the infinite is more accessible.
Knowing that spiritual development can occur during
creativity, Roethke comments that the intuitive leaps
are ". . . one of the ways man at least approaches the
divine--in this comprehensive act, the really good
poem" (SP 27).

   Not only is there a fundamental connection in
Roethke's poetry between the shape of the poetry and
the movement toward knowledge of the self, there is
also an affinity between the poetic discipline and the
spiritual process by which the journey of the self is
embedded in the poetry to become "essential action
outward" (8 #115). The mental processes employed in
the creative act resemble those practiced in the
religious quest.   Both endeavors are spiritual
disciplines guided by recollection and contemplation as
well as the faculties of memory, imagination,
intellect, and will. The poetic discipline creates a
meditative tendency in the mind, producing a poetry
which is naturally meditative in its structure and
themes. Thus the arts of poetry and meditation meet in
the creative act.   For Roethke this means that the
poetry becomes the form of meditation by which he seeks
"a reality more than the immediate" (SP 19).

   His purpose is suggested by these ideas juxtaposed
in a 1948 notebook entry: "Asceticism=absorb into /
Creativeness=forget self" (7 #267).   Roethke used
creativeness, the poetic act itself, as the mode of
asceticism by which he sought to forget the phenomenal

self and to find the deeper self. The central effort
in the poetry is "To find the self and then not escape
from it, but transcend it" (10 #137). It is not
surprising, then, that Arnold Stein, a colleague who
knew Roethke well, is convinced that "What
contemplation was to some philosophers, composition was
to Roethke."[10] A 1953 notebook entry, which is
actually a quotation from Jacques Maritain's Creative
Intuition in Art and Poetry, reveals that the poet was
aware of the virtues common to both activities:
"Fortitude, renouncement, obedience, order, humility
are aesthetic virtues in the realm of art, as they are
Christian virtues in the realm of moral life" (10
#142).[11] His dedication to his craft not only produced
a poetic asceticism preparatory for meditative poetry,
but also permitted him to achieve a sense of wholeness
amid the manic-depressive phases of his life. As Stein
has affirmed, Roethke ". . . could and did transform
his life in poetry."[12]

Roethke's belief that through the poetic act his
real life has been touched is emphasized in a 1949
notebook: "In my poems, there is much more reality
than in any relationship or affection that I feel; when
I create, I am true, and I would like to find the
strength to base my life entirely on this truth, on
this infinite simplicity and joy . . ." (8 #111).
Through the poetic discipline Roethke projects the self
on a mental stage, attempting to understand it and re-
create it in relation to the life of the spirit. This
protagonist is "not 'I,' personally," Roethke writes in
Twentieth Century Authors, but the "spiritual history.
. . of all haunted and harried men" (SP 15).
"Perpetual beginner," (3 #24) he plunges again and
again into the chaos, seeking through the explorations

of the dramatic personae to reshape the self and,
ultimately, to "transform this flesh to soul" (2
#10). The speaker's journey becomes not only Roethke's
journey but ours as well. As he comments in this 1949-
50 notebook entry, "If you don't like me, it's because
you don't like yourself, because my whole method is to
call you up and out" (8 #113). The method by which the
deeper self is called out is referred to by Roethke as
contemplation.

II

In a 1942 notebook entry Theodore Roethke
discloses the purpose of his art and the medium in
which he will work: "There are sources of life we must
reach: we must. I hope I have suggested to you the
necessity, the inevitability of contemplation" (3
#28). It would be difficult to find a more suitable
way to introduce Roethke's meditative poetry, for in
these lines the poet speaks fervently of the spiritual
quest that engenders the poetry and the corresponding
method which will guide the search. But Roethke's
comments do not explain the meaning of contemplation or
clarify the true nature of the journey. He provides an
additional hint in a 1951 entry when he speaks of "A
poetry of longing: not for escape, but for a greater
reality" (9 #123). The "greater reality" for which he
longs in the poetry becomes a quest for selfhood and a
search for God, explorations which are bound together
by the practice of contemplation and the meditative
discipline.

In order to understand more fully why Roethke is a
meditative poet, we must first define contemplation and
meditation and examine the nature of the contemplative
way, particularly as it is applied to Roethke's

poetry. The term contemplation is used in two distinct
ways in Evelyn Underhill's Mysticism, a work which
Roethke studied thoroughly. In its most general sense,
it is described as a power of perception available both
to the mystic and the artist: "a self-forgetting
attentiveness, a profound concentration, a self-
merging, which operates a real communion between the
seer and the seen" (M 300). It is the human faculty
which Underhill refers to in Practical Mysticism as
"ordinary contemplation,"   a natural form of the
contemplative consciousness not only accessible to all
individuals but one which is ". . . the essential
activity of all artist," poets and painters alike.[13] I
propose to show that this way of seeing, resulting in a
connection between the visible and invisible worlds, is
the foundation of Roethke's poetry and his mystical
view of reality.   As experienced by the mystic,
however, Contemplation is an extreme form of
introversion which establishes communion between the
soul and the Absolute. "Contemplation is the mystic's
medium," [her italics] the means by which a higher
level of consciousness is reached (M 299). It differs
from "ordinary" or "natural" contemplation by being a
deeper, purer form of contemplation which is passive
rather than active: the state of receptivity in which
Union with the All occurs.

Whereas natural contemplation is a way of seeing
accessible to anyone, the use of pure contemplation
requires education, "the gradual development of an
extraordinary faculty of concentration, a power of
spiritual attention" (M 300). "It is not enough, "
Underhill continues, "that he should naturally be
'aware of the Absolute,' unless he be able to
contemplate it" (M 300). For this reason Underhill

also uses the term <u>contemplation</u> broadly to encompass all the Degrees of Interior Prayer, beginning in Recollection or Meditation, merging into Quiet or Interior Silence, and culminating in mystical Contemplation. The goal of this process of introversion is union, which is a passive state, not the willed conditions of the earlier stages.

Roethke's awareness of the self's progress in contemplation is evident from this notebook entry in the early 1930's. His opening statements are drawn directly from footnotes in Underhill's <u>Mysticism</u>:

> St. Theresa Meditation, Quiet, nameless
>   intermediate, Orison of Union
> Hugh, St. Victor: Meditation, Soliloquy,
>   Consideration, Rapture
> The new silence upon me
> My first lesson too hard.
> St. Theresa: 1) meditation / / Stilled in
>   a whirlwind. (1 #8; Cf. <u>M</u> 309).

In addition to indicating Roethke's own practice of meditation, these notes point to the fact that mystics use different terminology in describing the phases of contemplation. Despite the confusion resulting from these various systems, we can see the typical progress from meditation to union. Roethke also records Underhill's detailed analysis of this continuous process of prayer in a 1957-58 notebook:

> Recollection begins in Meditation and
> develops into Orison of Inward Silence and
> Simplicity, which melts into true "Quiet."
> Quiet as it becomes deeper passes into
> Ordinary Contemplation: and this grows
> through Contemplation proper to Orison of
> Passive Union. (12 #172; Cf. <u>M</u> 309-310).

Instead of being stages of growth, these phases actually shade into and out of one another. We can also discern three forms of contemplation: Ordinary Contemplation, Contemplation proper, and that pure Contemplation resulting in Passive Union with Absolute Reality. We will delineate these forms in a later chapter when Roethke's poetry begins to reflect their use. For now we will consider them broadly as the achievement of levels of Reality: the world of Becoming, the world of Being, and that Absolute Reality wherein opposites are reconciled. The general progress of the self's education involves what the mystics refer to as the Purgative, Illuminative and Unitive Ways, a movement from meditation to contemplation to union.

Roethke's understanding of the method of contemplation as well as the obvious differences between the recollective (meditative) and contemplative states is found in the notebooks. He records this definition of meditation in a 1950 notebook, a passage which I have found to be a quotation from Evelyn Underhill's Practical Mysticism: "Meditation is a half-way house between thinking and contemplating: and as a discipline derives its chief value from this transitional character" (3 #117; cf. PM 46). Later, in a 1955 entry, it is obvious that he has been reading the chapter from Underhill's Mysticism on Introversion: Recollection and Quiet, for he indicates his own grasp of her discussion of the Degrees of Mental Prayer--the relationship between mysticism and prayer--followed by notes on Recollection and Contemplation:

Mysticism is just prayer: self-surrender to
    the author of our being.
Recollection: trains self   in   spiritual
    attention.
Contemplation: "Mental attitude under which
    all things give up to us the secret of
    their life."
    (12 #160; Cf. M 310-313, 301)

These broad definitions are supported by detailed notes
in the 1957-58 notebooks, including this summary of the
primary distinctions stated by Underhill:

Contemplation instills a method of being and
    knowing.
Meditation: one simple state;
The contemplative is merged like a bird in
    air
----
imageless
Who, knowing this, knows all;
    (13 #176; Cf. M 330, 332)

Viewed broadly, contemplation is the mental attitude
which permits one to penetrate the secret life of all
things. This is the method of ordinary contemplation
used by Roethke to achieve a "sacramental view of
nature" 5 #65). It is the "intensity in the seeing"
which he speaks of in "On 'Identity'": "To look at a
thing so long that you are a part of it and it is a
part of you. . ." (SP 25). As employed by the mystic,
Recollection is the practice of the awareness of God, a
simple psychic condition of concentration beginning in
meditation; contemplation proper is a more complex
state of being and knowing involving a union of
"thought, love, and will" (M 329). While Meditation is
the discipline of spiritual attention in which mystical

prayer begins, pure Contemplation is the method which produces the imageless merging of the self with Absolute Reality. Roethke's use of the word "imageless" is important, for in her analysis of the Degrees of Interior Prayer Underhill discusses the movement toward Union as a change from the perception of Reality as a symbol to the experience of the Absolute in imageless revelation.

This change in perception is central to an understanding of the development of the mystic consciousness and thus the contemplative way. It is a psychological change which marks the spiritual growth of the contemplative between the Prayer of Quiet and mystical Contemplation. The entire journey, known as the Mystic Way, progresses in five stages: Awakening, Purification of the Self, Illumination, Dark Night of the Soul, and Union. The interior process implied in this journey involves an arduous search for the transcendent faculty, the deepest center of the self. The superficial self, the ego, is transmuted and the deeper self, the "inner I," emerges to undergo the steps toward union. Once this true self is allowed to live, Union with the Absolute is possible. The implication of the pathway is that the contemplative life is not achieved, or shall we say does not begin, until this Union is realized in love. That is, only when the full mystic consciousness has been attained is the contemplative way completed. The level of prayer attained by the contemplative depends upon the degree of love residing in the soul as well as a willingness to surrender the self to the All.

Roethke speaks of the true self in a 1942 notebook as one who "lives on a higher, a nobler level" (3 #28). He comments further on the essential character

of the spiritual search in a 1946 entry, employing the
language of the writer of De Adhaerando Deo quoted by
Underhill: "Paradox: 'To mount to God is to enter
into one's self'" (8 #112; Cf. M 304). Paradoxically,
then, the way down is the way up: the interior journey
and the movement of the soul toward God are the same.
Roethke even queries in another 1946 notebook, "God is
a point in the deepest self?" (6 #88). Distinctions
between inward and outward become blurred and cease to
exist. What may appear to be a movement in two
directions is actually a single process.

To place Roethke in the meditative tradition
implies that he employs ordinary contemplation to
attain a consciousness of the Absolute immanent in the
natural world and that he strives to reach the sources
of life, the deeper self and God, which is the ground
of the universe. We should remember, however, that the
highest form of contemplation, "infused" contemplation,
cannot be attained by striving: it is given through
grace. The quest revealed in Roethke's poetry begins
in a search of the self for identity and culminates in
"a hunt, a drive toward God" in the "Sequence,
Sometimes Metaphysical."[14] Each of the major sequences
is a meditation on some aspect of this journey, a
progress by which the poet "would stretch in both
directions, like the root and branch of a tree" (10
#135). His aim is to know the self and then transcend
it, to stretch beyond the self toward the natural world
and God, achieving in the end a sense of unity and
joy. Roethke's poetry may be viewed broadly, then, as
a meditation upon man and his search for wholeness, an
effort to attain selfhood--a sense of spiritual
identity. As the poetry evolves, the deeper self
emerges and Roethke's speaker experiences a sense of

wholeness by which he participates in the cosmic dance
of the universe and feels that "Body and soul are
one!."[15] By embracing the periods of revelation and
uncertainty, the poetry progresses toward a self which
accepts its finiteness, surrenders its will to know,
and runs joyously "toward a Hill" exclaiming in
adoration, "More! O More! visible" (CP 251).

                              III

        Since Roethke has commented that "Mysticism is
just prayer: self-surrender to the author of our
being," (12 #160) a consideration of the level of
mental prayer attained in the poetry must incorporate a
discussion of the Mystic Way.   As indicated earlier,
the mystic arrives at the moment of passive Union with
Divine Reality by employing Recollection (Meditation),
Quiet, and Contemplation, the states of mental prayer,
to discipline the faculties.   These Degrees of Interior
Prayer correspond roughly to the steps of the Mystic
Way outlined above.   Both pathways represent a
continuous, orderly growth.   In practice, however, many
mystics reverse or even omit one or more of the phases
of education.   We should be cautious, therefore, not to
be too rigid in identifying the stages in the
process.   Though there is an obvious problem in
relating the threefold and fivefold ways, an
approximation can be reached.   Underhill prefers to
compare the development of prayer to the Purgative,
Illuminative, and Unitive Ways.   We should be mindful,
however, that the relationship is inexact and some
overlapping may occur.   Accordingly, the initial state
of Recollection or Meditation may involve Awakening and
Purification of the Self; the Prayer of Quiet may
exhibit characteristics of Purgation and Illumination

of the Self; and Contemplation may be an experience of
the Dark Night of the Soul which leads to Union with
Reality. When this schema is compared with Underhill's
three forms of contemplation, we find that Ordinary
Contemplation is the valid seeing which occurs during
Illumination; Contemplation proper leads to the Dark
Night of the Soul; and pure Contemplation produces the
soul's mystical Union with Reality.

Roethke's poetry reflects this journey of the self
but it is dominated by the initial steps of the Mystic
Way: Awakening, Purification, and Illumination of the
Self. Dark Night of the Soul and Union, the mark of
the contemplative, occur only rarely in Roethke's later
poetry. I would argue, therefore, that the poetry is
more appropriately termed "meditative" rather than
"mystical."[16] To clarify this distinction we must look
more closely at the Degrees of Interior Prayer and
their relationship to the Mystic Way. As stated
earlier, Recollection or Meditation is the first state
of mental prayer that leads gradually to the stage of
Quiet or Interior Silence and merges finally into
mystical Contemplation. Though the methods of
meditation and contemplation are different, the two
terms have been used interchangeably during their
history, no doubt because they have been difficult to
distinguish except as extremes of a gradual life-
process.[17] Nevertheless, distinctions have been drawn,
particularly by Underhill. These variations in meaning
and practice are important as a framework for an
analysis of Roethke's meditative poetry.

Recollection, defined by Underhill as "a
collecting or gathering in of the attention of the self
to its 'most hidden cell,'" is a psychic condition
which begins in meditation (M 314). By ignoring the

external world, while at the same time keeping the
faculties awake, the contemplative concentrates upon a
visual image, thus producing a willed state of
consciousness which is "a half-way house between the
perception of appearance and the perception of Reality"
(M 315). Underhill emphasizes that in this meditative
state, the self "still feels very clearly the edge of
its own personality; its separateness from the Somewhat
Other, the divine reality set over against the soul"
(M 315). The self is aware of that reality but does
not experience, as in pure contemplation, a fusion with
the All. In the recollective state, the subject of
meditation is still "a symbol through which it [the
self] receives a distinct message from the
transcendental world" (M 315). Unlike the mystics,
Roethke's speakers open themselves to the natural world
rather than withdrawing from it, thereby seeing the
transcendent immanent in the world. Their moment of
illumination, however, is similar to that of the
mystics. It breaks in upon the consciousness, usually
in the form of an awareness of the presence of the
Eternal or a sense of regeneration after they have
worked through their anxiety.

The Prayer of Quiet or Simplicity is a state which
entails stripping the self of the "I" and simplifying
or purifying its intentions in order to surrender
itself in love to a higher Reality. This process
involves a further withdrawal of the senses from the
external world, an emptying of the field of
consciousness so that it can be filled by the
Absolute. During this transitional phase, however, the
contemplative is still conscious of its own
personality. The self-cleansing prepares for, or in
some instances may even begin the union of the soul

with Pure Being, merely by the fact that the soul is
more receptive, yet the soul is still waiting for union
to be completed. Underhill states that this psychic
state is "the intellectual complement and expression of
the moral state of humility and receptivity: the very
condition, says Eckhart, of the new Birth" (M 319).
The Prayer of Quiet is viewed by Underhill as a gateway
to mystical Contemplation; therefore, she maintains
that though it "is a common condition of mystical
attainment, it is not by itself mystical at all"
(M 324). Only when the full mystic consciousness has
evolved can the contemplative life be realized in the
Union of love.

The highest stage of interior prayer, pure
Contemplation, is characterized by Underhill in
Practical Mysticism as a change from "active" to
"infused" or "passive" contemplation (PM 123-25).
Heretofore, the mind and the will have been actively
pursuing Reality, but now, as Underhill states, the
contemplative should "cease all conscious, anxious
striving and pushing" (PM 125). In this deep
contemplation, the self abandons its character to
another center, surrendering itself in love to the will
and activity of God. During this period of submission
and receptivity the soul is united with Divine Reality
which Underhill describes as "a union of love, a glad
and humble self-mergence in the universal life"
(PM 127). The soul moves beyond multiplicity to a
sense of Simplicity or oneness, beyond self-
consciousness to be merged with the consciousness of
the Whole. Ultimately, the field of consciousnes is
widened and deepened so that the contemplative passes
"beyond the cosmic experience to the personal
encounter, the simple yet utterly inexpressible union

of the soul with its God" (PM 139). Having transcended
the world of sense and time, the contemplative rests in
a state of Being.

This study will show that Roethke's poetry
touches the state of Recollection described by
Underhill and transcends it to depict a form of Quiet;
only in the final sequence does it push beyond this
state to explore mystical Contemplation, producing an
experience of union which seems willed rather than
infused. The struggle to come near to God presented in
the "Sequence, Sometimes Metaphysical" is a "hunt," a
"drive," not the passive receptivity described by
mystics who have attained Union with Reality. In my
view, then, the poetry reveals states which Underhill
calls "conditions of mystical experience," but which
she cautions are not by themselves mystical at all (M
324). Though certain passages in the poetry may be
termed "mystical," we should be careful not to label
the entire corpus of the poetry mystical, nor argue
that it is, therefore, the product of true mystical
experience resulting in pure contemplation. It is more
accurate to note the mystical elements in the poetry
but to use the term "meditative" in describing the mode
in which Roethke creates and the levels of
consciousness manifested in the poetry. Though
Roethke's notebooks indicate that he longed to attain
the mystic consciousness, the poetry is dominated by
the lower states of prayer: Meditation
(Awakening/Purification) and Quiet (Purgation/
Illumination). It is more appropriate, therefore, to
view Roethke as a meditative poet whose poetry is
infused with mystical thought and with the mystical
structures he had learned through his careful reading
of Underhill, et al.

Roethke's readings in mystical literature will be used as a framework for analyzing his meditative sequences. In addition to Underhill's Mysticism, Roethke read St. Francis de Sales' Introduction to a Devout Life, the mystical treatise The Cloud of Unknowing, Underhill's Practical Mysticism, Dean William Inge's Christian Mysticism, Nicolas Berdyaev's Freedom and the Spirit, and two works by Rudolf Otto, The Idea of the Holy and Mysticism East and West. Since numerous quotations from the writings of Meister Eckhart are included in Roethke's Notebooks, I have also employed Eckhart when such an approach seemed appropriate. By applying this literature rather than more contemporary studies of mysticism, I have endeavored to be true to the sources of Roethke's understanding of the mystic way, particularly its use of meditation and contemplation.

IV

In arguing that Roethke is a poet in the meditative tradition, I am not claiming that he is a devotional poet as were the seventeenth century poets of the genre, such a Donne, Herbert and Vaughan. Roethke's poems are not instruments of his faith; nor may they properly be called spiritual exercises. They are not devotional lyrics whose aim is to quicken the spirit in diligent obedience to God and active charity toward others. Rather than charting the progress of the soul toward salvation, they reveal the purgative stretchings of the self to become a soul and the attendant struggles of the soul to know God. It is in the inward-and-outward motion of the soul--the stretching and striving of the self to become a spiritual entity--that these modern poems assume the

character and grace of spiritual exercises of the
sixteenth and seventeenth centuries. Their purpose is
not to transform the speaker's life in love and service
to Jesus Christ and the Church. Sin does not shake
Roethke's speakers, nor is freedom found in total
submission to God. Spiritual malaise, death, and a
desire to know God move Roethke's protagonists, while a
sense of freedom comes from attaining spiritual
identity and dancing amid the created things of God's
universe. Like Vaughan, Roethke seeks and finds the
eternal in the natural world; rarely, however, does he
depict the inner presence of God in the soul. Nor does
he share Herbert's struggle between the lure of this
world and God's call to absolute obedience. Instead of
being tortured by sin and the world, Roethke's speakers
strive to create the true self, one that is in harmony
with itself and the natural world. The attachment to
the divine expressed in the poetry of Herbert and Donne
is replaced in Roethke's poetry by an agonizing search
for unity of self and knowledge of the eternal.

Roethke's poetry pushes toward God, but it is not
a meditation by which the self is conformed to the
principles of Jesus Christ, thereby attaining salvation
and happiness. Roethke was reared a Presbyterian, but
as he says in the notebooks, he "went to Sunday school
and acquired an active loathing for Jesus Christ as
conceived by the pastors" (4 #52). Throughout his life
he remained "a contender, a wrestler with God" (3 #37)
and apparently never became reconciled to Jesus
Christ. In a 1944 entry he explains "Why I hate
Christ?--Because feminine" (5 #64) and he omits Jesus
from the trinity in a 1962 entry, wondering "Have I
made my own trinity--The God, the Holy Ghost . . . ?"
(14 #208). Though Roethke's thought is incomplete, the

passage indicates that he considered God and the Holy
spirit central to the Godhead, not Jesus Christ.   It
would be inappropriate, then, to view Roethke as a
Christian poet who is writing devotional poetry.   He
does not compose hymns to God, meditations on the life
of Christ and sin, or theological explorations of the
relationship between body and soul.   Nevertheless,
Roethke's concerns--the themes which he has stated in
"On 'Identity'"--are religious concerns; and as such,
they are no less intense, personal or valid for our
time than the devotional concerns of the seventeenth
century meditative poets.

Roethke's general themes are appropriate to a
modern poet who has experienced self-consciousness, the
disorder of modern existence, and separation from
God.   "I take it that we are faced with at least four
principal themes," Roethke says in "On 'Identity'":

> (1) The multiplicity, the chaos of modern
> life; (2) The way, the means of establishing
> a personal identity, a self in the face of
> that chaos (3) The nature of creation, that
> faculty for producing order out of disorder
> in the arts, particularly in poetry; and (4)
> The nature of God Himself. (SP 19)

These themes do not merely coexist in the poetry; they
converge to constitute its whole movement.   Roethke
uses the creative process to explore the nature of the
self and God, thereby moving beyond multiplicity to
simplicity which is manifested as unity of self and
union with the universe.   As I discussed earlier, the
movement toward knowledge of the self as well as the
inner and outer reality of the world is inherent in the
creative act itself.   Such knowledge is essential to
the creative spirit and the working of poetic

intuition.   Roethke's exploration of the nature of
creation is simultaneously the journey to the center of
the soul, the struggle for self-identity, and the
effort to transcend the self.   Thus the themes coalesce
in the poetry to produce order out of chaos.

Roethke's poetry is not exclusively Christian, as
were the lyrics of the seventeenth century meditative
poets, yet it shares characteristics common to the
meditative genre.   It records the struggle to create
the true self and, as this analysis proposes to show,
the movement of the major sequences resembles the
traditional meditative structure.   Moreover, the levels
of consciousness attained by Roethke's speakers are
normally below the stage of "infused" or passive
contemplation, necessitating that the poetry be termed
"meditative"   rather   than   "mystical."   Roethke's
meditations also share in the broad concerns of the
genre, notably the relationship between the body and
the soul, the self and God, in the progress toward
illumination.   Though his lyrics may not properly be
called devotional prayers, they often contain petition
and praise within them and the poetry as a whole drives
toward God.   The key elements in the meditative process
linking Roethke to the earlier poets in the tradition
are the use of natural contemplation and self-
analysis.   Roethke's speakers address the self more
often than God, yet their moments. of illumination as
well as their efforts to approach God are as authentic
as the mode of the seventeenth century poets.

                                V

The primary mark of the meditative poet is his
practice of the meditative discipline, a mental
attitude which not only influences the creative act but
also governs the psychological and structural patterns

of the poetry. Roethke's concern with the stress of
the psyche during the spiritual journey is indicative
of the modern poem in the meditative tradition. In The
Poetry of Meditation, Louis L. Martz presents this
broad definition of the meditative poem:

> a work what creates an interior drama of the
> mind; this dramatic action is usually (though
> not always) created by some form of self-
> address, in which the mind grasps firmly a
> problem or situation deliberately evoked by
> the memory, brings it forward toward the full
> light of consciousness, and concludes with a
> moment of illumination, where the speaker's
> self has, for a time, found an answer to its
> condition.[18]

The result of this interior drama, Martz adds, is the
creation of the self: "A self that is, ideally, one
with itself, with other human beings, with created
nature, and with the supernatural."[19] This process of
meditation is the movement of the interior dramas found
in Roethke's major sequences, each composed of five or
more long poems in which a speaker journeys out of
chaos into light. As the sequences develop, the
speakers are aided in confronting their spiritual
conditions by the powers of the soul: memory,
intellect, and will.[20] These agents guide the speakers
in resolving their inner conflicts, assisting them in
progressing from self-searching to a moment of
certitude. Not all of Roethke's speakers attain the
ideal described by Martz, but most achieve
self-integration and experience the eternal in the
natural world. Only in the final sequence does the
drive toward God produce a sense of active union with
the Godhead. The pattern of Awakening, Purification,

and Illumination of the Self recurs in the poetry, for the creation of the self is a life-task. It should be no surprise, then, that Roethke is a perpetual beginner: the inner self re-emerges as the poetry evolves. Not until the end of the poetry does the "true self" appear to dance with Bird, Leaf, Fish and Snail following a dark night of the soul (CP 251).

The mental processes which prepare the speaker for the moment of illumination reflect those practiced by St. Francis de Sales and St. Ignatius of Loyola. Roethke's method of meditation is less formal, more associative, yet the general meditative process is the same. The broad structure of meditative poetry has been outlined by Louis L. Martz in this manner:

> Without expecting any hard and fast divisions, then, we should expect to find a formal meditation falling into three distinguishable portions, corresponding to the acts of memory, understanding, and will-- portions which we might call composition, analysis, and colloquy.[21]

The internal structure of the disciplines of St. Francis de Sales and St. Ignatius is more exact, of course. St. Francis recommends a procedure involving preparations, considerations, spiritual acts and resolutions, concluding with colloquies of thanksgiving, offerings, and petitions.[22] St. Ignatius implores the penitent to use a preparatory prayer, two preludes, three principal points, and a colloquy; later in the Spiritual Exercises he expands the Meditation to include three preludes, five points, and three colloquies.[23] Despite slight variations, these meditative structures are the same: they include composition (imagination and memory), analysis

(intellect or understanding), and colloquy (will). A
closer examination of these disciplines will be useful
for the analysis of the meditative process inherent in
Roethke's sequences.

     To prepare for mental prayer, St. Francis
explains, "The first thing is to place yourself in the
presence of God and ask his help." Following this
request for inspiration, it is often useful, he adds,
"to represent to the imagination the scene of the
mystery you are considering as if it were actually
taking place before you." Once the imagination is
invoked in this preparatory part, the penitent employs
"understanding, and this is what we call meditation; in
other words, making use of considerations to raise your
heart to God and to the things of God." These
analytical discourses lead the meditator to form a
complete understanding of the mystery or subject.
"Meditation ultimately moves our will," St. Francis
states, "to make spiritual acts such as the love of God
and our neighbour," and "to make practical resolutions
according to your special needs." He recommends that
these be made by using colloquies which, address the
Lord, the saints, ourselves, or even inanimate
creatures.[24] Thus, St. Francis' devotional meditation
develops logically according to memory, understanding
and will. He believes it is necessary for the
imagination and the intellect to guide and inform the
soul before the will can produce action resulting in
utterances of thanksgiving and petition.

     St. Ignatius also indicates that the meditation is
made with "the three powers of the soul," and that the
preparatory prayer consists of two preludes: forming
"a mental image of the place" and asking "God our Lord
for what I want and desire" to achieve in the entire

exercise. All three powers of the soul--memory, understanding, and will--are employed in analyzing the major points or divisions of the subject under contemplation, and the prayer closes with a colloquy or conversation with Christ, "speaking as one friend speaks to another, or as a servant speaks to his master. . . making known his affairs to Him and seeking His advice concerning them."[25]

The movement of Roethke's meditative sequences follows this general pattern of development, using composition, analysis, and colloquy. Internally, however, they are distinct from the meditations of St. Francis and St. Ignatius. The self is usually addressed, not God; the second prelude is sometimes omitted; and the powers of the soul are not employed in a rigid fashion. Memory often aids in analysis as well as in composition and at times all three powers are active in the colloquy. Moreover, Roethke's poetic technique is freer and more spontaneous than the design outlined above suggests. As he states in a 1947 notebook entry: "The method is to use the mind in a state of dissociation: rush of images, with a condensation of meaning" (2 #12). The images of memory and the explorations of meaning lead, ultimately, to the moment of illumination. For the poet this moment is the culmination of meditative discipline. Roethke comments on this process in a 1956-57 notebook: "The instantaneous enlightenment, the paradoxical leap out of time is obtained after a long discipline which comprises a philosophy as well as a mystical technique" (12 #172). All of these mental processes-- recollection, understanding, and enlightenment--create Roethke's meditative sequences. We must remember, however, that they always open with the mind and soul

in a state of crisis. Moreover, the movement of the
speaker's soul from anguish to illumination is finally
more important than any system of meditation or form of
contemplation. While I propose to demonstrate that
Roethke's sequences develop according to this
fundamental organization, it is equally important to
stress the progress of the speakers toward the creation
of the true self. Both of these organizing impulses
are at the root of Roethke's meditative poetry. They
function in a natural, spontaneous way, not as a
rigorous discipline consciously employed by the poet.

II

The *LOST SON SEQUENCE*

Roethke's first interior drama is the <u>Lost Son Sequence</u>, a cycle of long poems, each of which he considered complete in itself and yet "a stage in a kind of struggle out of the slime; part of a slow spiritual progress; an effort to be born, and later, to become something more" (<u>SP</u> 37). This meditative sequence traces "the spiritual history of a protagonist (not 'I' personally, but of all haunted and harried men") (<u>SP</u> 10). To communicate the journey, Roethke employs rhythms which "catch the very movement of the mind itself" (<u>SP</u> 10), beginning "from the viewpoint of a very small child" and progressing toward sexual and spiritual awareness (<u>SP</u> 41). The entire struggle Roethke states in "Open Letter," is composed of "a succession of experiences, similar yet dissimilar. There is a perpetual slipping-back, then a going-forward; but there is some 'progress'" (<u>SP</u> 39). Roethke comments further on the process in a 1947 notebook:

> It is an advance and a regression. After each episode, each poem, it would seem that I have slipped back into the pit; but it isn't the same pit; it's another and a bit further up on the spiral ascent, though still a part of the marshy plains. What happens is in some ways the same.
>
> ----------
>
> my mind tired: a psychic exhaustion
>
> (7 #100)

The sequence is governed, then, by a cyclical pattern of progression-regression-progression, creating a

spiral effect. This pattern recurs throughout the
poetry as well, for as Roethke explains,
"Disassociation often precedes a new state of clarity"
(SP 41). The moments of illumination are repeated, but
they vary in intensity, each advancing the protagonist
closer to self-identity and to the apprehension of a
"reality more than the immediate" (SP 19).

In discussing the process involved in creating the
sequence, Roethke emphasizes that the poet works
"intuitively" so that the "final form of the poem" is
"imaginatively right"; "the 'meaning' itself should
come as a dramatic revelation, an excitement":

> I believe that, in this kind of poem,
> the poet, in order to be true to what is
> most universal in himself, should not
> rely on allusion; should not comment or
> employ many judgement words; should not
> meditate (or maunder). He must scorn
> being "mysterious" or loosely oracular,
> but be willing to face up to genuine
> mystery. His lanquage must be
> compelling and immediate: he must
> create an actuality (SP 42).

The final poem is dramatic and immediate, "with the
mood or the action on the page, not talked-about, not
the meditative, T.S. Eliot kind of thing" (SL 122).
Instead of creating "reflective" poetry with "too much
talk," as does "Eliot in the Quartets," Roethke
believes that spiritual history should be rendered by
"dramatic poetry" (SL 142). Only in this way will he
be able to "create an actuality."

In order to represent the actual experience--the
sense of immediacy of a spiritual crisis--the poet must
undergo an interior journey to the self hidden in the

spiritual unconscious. Roethke explained this process
when he applied to the Yaddo Foundation for funding to
expand the sequence. He had written "The Lost Son",
"The Long Alley", and "The Shape of the Fire", but felt
he had not "exhausted the theme: I wish to go beyond
these poems. This means going into myself more deeply
and objectifying more fully what I find, probably in a
dramatic poem that could be staged" (SL 126). By going
more deeply into himself, the poet touches poetic
intuition and the subjectivity of the self.

Poetic intuition, Maritain states, is "both
creative and cognitive"; it is creative "with respect
to the engendering of the work" and cognitive "with
respect to what is grasped by it."[1] Since what is
grasped by poetic intuition is "the singular existence
which resounds in the subjectivity of the poet,
together with all the other realities which echo in
this existence," the work it does--the created poem--
will be "both a revelation of the subjectivitiy of the
poet and of the reality that poetic knowledge has
caused him to perceive."[2] The poem, then, is not only
"poetic intuition come to objectivization," it is also
"a sign--both a direct sign of the secrets perceived in
things . . . and a reversed sign of the subjective
universe of the poet, of his substantial Self obscurely
revealed."[3]

Once poetic intuition is born in the unconscious,
moved by the spontaneous stirrings of the soul, it
seeks knowledge of natural things and the deepest
self. It is this knowledge--the content of poetic
intuition--that is expressed in the poem. Born in the
unconscious of the spirit, poetic intuition proceeds
through the imagination to the intellect and becomes
the "intellective flash" from which the poet creates--

an object and a sign of his whole being.[4] In apparent
belief that the poem represents the unity of the poet,
Roethke states in "On Identity'": "When I was young,
to make something in language, a poem that was all of a
piece, a poem that could stand for what I was at the
time--that seemed to be the most miraculous thing in
the world" (SP 27).

The working of poetic intuition is a spontaneous,
free activity in the depths of the soul where
imagination, intellect, and all the other powers of the
soul abide in union. Moving deeper into the soul, the
poet meets this radiating unity, poetic knowledge is
grasped, and the poem comes into being. As the soul's
powers function naturally in the poet so they emerge
spontaneously into the poem. If Roethke intends, then,
to trace the spiritual and psychological history of a
protagonist, the powers of the soul--memory,
understanding and will--will be at work in the poem
even as they are the activating agents in the creative
process. Each effort--poetic knowledge and the poem
itself--is initiated by recollection or meditation, and
each in its final form is a unified whole, representing
the soul's powers and thus the poet himself.

The six poems usually considered to be the first
part of the Lost Son Sequence were published in Praise
to the End! in 1951. In my view, these poems serve as
an introduction to the meditative cycle in which the
protagonist employs the powers of the soul--memory
(imagination), understanding (intellect) and will--to
journey from the dark cave to the field of light. In
these initial poems, however, Roethke uses the language
and associative skills of a child's mind to "create the
'as if' of the child's world" (SP 41). The words and
rhythms of the poems render the child's increasing

awareness of the body and the external world--an
experience in which we all have participated: the
universal becomes immediate. The journey into the
depths of the self to create the child's effort to be
born touches the racial unconscious, producing
archetypal images of physical and emotional pain
associated with birth, life, death of the father and
God, sexual and spiritual potency, and questions of
eternal life. Roethke's images are at once sexual and
spiritual. As he observes in a 1944-45 notebook, "In
myself I feel a great duel between the spiritual and
the sensual developing" (5 #65). This duel is
expressed throughout the sequence, even in the
meditative cycle, but ultimately Roethke considered the
poems to be spiritual:

> Agent of purgation, attend me.
>
> ----------
>
> I'm in the pits still; in the mire,
> spiritually. I can't seem to throw off
> the sensuality that is so much a part of
> me. I don't want to throw it off. I'm
> not tempted; I'm a temptor [sic]. Maybe
> I'm of the party of the Devil. One of
> his sedusors [sic]; fat danger.
>
> ----------
>
> I conceive of them as spiritual poems:
> I wonder if you do, or whether you think
> them rough--painfully explicit, a mere
> wallow in sensuality. (5 #65)

Though there are both obvious and obsure sexual images
in the sequence, the progress of the son is toward
spiritual awakening and an acceptance of the whole of
life, particularly the relationship of body and soul,
the self and the light.

In the six poems which create the child's world,
Roethke focuses on what the child sees, hears and
feels, as well as on his ability to name himself, to
figure out what he is in relation to elements in the
natural world, and to know his body, to be aware that
he is becoming somebody else. Equally important in the
child's development is his experience of pain and
guilt: a kitten and his parents "biting" him; his
father dying; and his fear of retribution after "I
fell!   I fell!" (CP 73). The fall may be,
metaphorically, original sin as well as his sense of
the father's displeasure with his "happy hands," the
hands with which he explores the body. On the physical
level the child's experiences progress from "I hear
flowers" to the need for love, not "No and Yes"; beyond
"Touch and arouse. Suck and sob" to a moment when he
insists "I am" (CP 73-82). Before he stands, "almost a
tree," and becomes a "tree beginning to know," he
undergoes spiritual development as well (CP 78-79).
When his father dies, he says "One father is enough. /
Maybe God has a house. / But not here" (CP 74). Later
the ground cries his name when he sees "a beard in a
cloud," but the "Love" that "helps the sun" is "not
enough" for the son separated from his father and
God. At the end of the fourth poem, "Give Way, Ye
Gates," he still bears his aloneness:

> The deep stream remembers:
> Once I was a pond.
> What slides away
> Provides. (CP 80)

The stream may remember its source, the origin of its
depth and expansion, but for the lost son the father
and God no longer provide. They are no longer supreme
authorities in his life. In the sixth poem, "O Lull

Me, Lull Me," knock and need, the gateways of the
senses, give way to the possibility of thinking and the
expression of "A wish!   A wish!"--the opening of the
intellect and the will.   "Is it time to think?" he asks
(CP 83).   Once he "could say hello to things" and "talk
to a snail," but now he is "all ready to whistle" and
he can "see what sings!":   "I'm more than when I was
born" (CP 84).   He defines himself as "crazed and
graceless, / A winter-leaping frog" (CP 83); "But I
can't go leaping alone," he says (CP 84).   This is the
wish: to do more than "see my heart in the seed"
(CP 83) and "see what sings!" (CP 84).   He desires not
to go leaping alone.   At this stage in his growth he
has become familiar with his body and the natural world
and is prepared to begin using the powers of the soul
"to become something more."   During the meditative
cycle he encounters light in the field, recovers the
aid of his father (God), and learns that "We never
enter / Alone" (CP 93).   The journey itself, the
struggle from the mire, teaches him that "This flesh
has airy bones" (CP 99).

   It is at this point, I would argue, that the
unified sequence begins, for only in the next eight
poems do the soul's powers function to create a cycle
of poems structured according to the progress of the
mind from composition to analysis to colloquy.   The
individual poems as well as the entire sequence follow
this general pattern of development.   Considered as a
sequence, the poems form a natural three-part
structure: composition--"The Lost Son" and "The Long
Alley"; analysis--"A Field of Light," "The Shape of
Fire," and "Praise to the End!"; colloquy--"Unfold!
Unfold!,"   "I Cry, Love!   Love!" and "O, Thou
Opening, O."   "A Light Breather," which Roethke called

the epilogue to the sequence (SL 161), comments on the
thematic movement of the meditation, summarizing the
essential nature of the son's journey. By outlining
this mental process, I am not suggesting that the
powers of the soul--memory (imagination), understanding
(intellect), and will--are aligned with this
arrangement in a strict manner. The poet works
intuitively and, therefore, the soul's powers may
overlap in aiding the son to resolve his inner
struggle. The dramatic action, as Roethke explains, is
"often implied or indicated in the interior monologue
or dialogue between the self and its mentor, or
conscience, or, sometimes, another person" (SP 10).
Thus the entire sequence is an interior monologue or
colloquy. The drama itself involves a movement out of
"the mire, the Void" (SP 40), as Roethke puts it in
"Open Letter," through several phases of spiritual
growth until the son knows "The flesh has airy bones"
(CP 99). Body and soul become one and he "can leap,
true to the field" (CP 98).

In a letter to Kenneth Burke, Roethke refers to "A
series of three longish poems about a mental and
spiritual crisis, "commenting that the first is "The
Lost Son" (SL 114). Subsequently, he states his belief
that "One must go back into the consciousness of the
race itself not just the quandries [sic] of
adolescence . . ." (SL 116). His purpose, stated in
"Open Letter," is "To begin from the depths and come
out"--all part of the effort not only to be born, but
to "become something more" (SP 40). The poet's journey
into the depths of the unconscious permits him to
communicate the archetypal images of fear, guilt,
aloneness, death and rebirth, images which are both
physical (sexual) and spiritual. The son is "lost"

because he is experiencing the sense of separation from his father and God, a feeling of guilt and unworthiness expressed in the frenzied running of the son who does not know which way to turn. For the poet, as for the lost son, only by going deep into the self can he understand and come to Be--to experience wholeness, the union of body and soul.

"The Lost Son," composed of five poems, prepares for the son's journey and thus the entire sequence by rendering the setting, the mood and even the questions which speak of the son's agony. In Ignatian terms this poem functions as the first prelude of the meditative sequence, usually referred to as composition of place, creating "a mental image of the place": "seeing with the mind's eye the physical place where the object that we wish to contemplate is present."[5] The meditator will always concentrate on an image appropriate to the subject matter of the meditation, whether the subject is visible or invisible. Roethke employs this general technique, but changes and expands it for his own poetic purposes according to the images and themes of the lost son's plight. The son's spiritual state is dramatized in the first poem, "The Flight," by depicting him "At Woodlawn" where he "heard the dead cry" and "shook the softening chalk of [his] bones" (CP 52). His condition is reiterated in the last poem by placing the character in "beginning winter, / An in-between time" and hearing him describe the brown landscape with its dead weeds swaying in the wind (CP 58). Roethke's statement in a 1944-45 notebook emphasizes the nature of the lost son's world:

> A brown field, dusted with snow, turns
> to a light yellow. An in-between time,
> before the complete harsh glittering
>   whiteness:
> A purgatorial world, a netherworld.
>   (5 #68)

Spiritually, he struggles in a purgatorial state. Knowing that he is lost, the protagonist cries out for help, at first to the snail, bird, worm, and then to the voices:

> Tell me:
> Which is the way I take;
> Out of what door do I go,
> Where and to whom? (CP 54).

This plea, though it is not a prayer to God, is one example of the Roethkean mode of petition, a request for guidance. The son calls to the snail to "glisten me forward" and asks the bird to "soft-sigh me home" (CP 53). The search, as Roethke says in "On Identity,'" is for "some clue to existence from the sub-human," but the protagonist "sees and yet does not see: they are almost tail-flicks, from another world, seen out of the corner of the eye" (SP 38). "Dark hollows" and the moon respond, giving neither answers nor comfort. The son's frantic search continues: "Running lightly over spongy ground," "Hunting along the river" (CP 54).

In the analytical portion of the poem, the son's questions indicate the other direction of this quest: "Who put the moss there?"--"Who stunned the dirt into noise?"--"Hath the rain a father?" (CP 55-56). He would search the depths and the heights but "All the caves are ice" (CP 56). He is not only lost, but cold and afraid: "Fear was my father, Father Fear"

(CP 56). Having "married [his] hands to perpetual agitation" by running "to the whistle of money," he admits that he is "falling through a dark swirl" (CP 56-57). The son persists naively in accepting the material rather than the invisible as real, thereby falling into the dark. Suddenly a memory returns as if in a dream, a double memory of the pipes knocking as the heating system is turned on in the greenhouse and of Papa coming, tapping his pipe as he walks. With the coming of warmth and "Papa"--"the papa on earth and heaven are blended, of course" (SP 39)--"The rose, the chrysanthemum turned toward the light" that moves "slowly over the white / Snow" (CP 57). This movement prepares for the first moment of illumination in "beginning winter" when the son sees light moving across "the frozen field," the brown landscape of dead weeds.

Suddenly the light and the wind stop, and then his mind moves, "not alone, / Through the clear air, in the silence":

Was it light?
Was it light within?
Was it light within light?
Stillness becoming alive,
Yet still? (CP 58)

Although the lost son is unable to explain the nature of the illumination, he nevertheless wonders if it is the paradoxical "light within light." The experience of light is too vague and tentative to suggest any notion of God, despite the fact that the mind moves "not alone." Roethke insisted in a long letter to Babette Deutsch that "the illumination is still only partly apprehended; he [the hero] is still 'waiting'" (SL 141).

A lively understandable spirit
Once entertained you.
It will come again.
Be still.
Wait. (CP 58)

This waiting is not a permanent condition, however; it
is rooted in and therefore strengthened by the son's
hope that the light will be restored. Until that time,
the lost son practices "seminal states of waiting and
watching, listening to winter wind-sounds, looking at
snow in the far-away field"--the modes of perception
characteristic of the poet's "sacramental view of
nature" (5 #65).

Composition of place continues in "The Long
Alley," but the poem also serves as a second prelude to
the meditative cycle. The protagonist regresses to the
point where "A river glides out of the grass. A river
or a serpent" and "The Dark flows on itself" (CP 59).
"My gates are all caves," he says. The glimmer of
light has vanished, "the bones mourn," and all doors
have become caves. The "sulphurous water" insinuates
that "The smoke's from the glory of God," but he "can't
name it" (CP 59). Since "The dead don't hurry," he
will glide slowly in, ferretting out "Who else breathes
here" (CP 59). The graves of the dead are still close.

The second prelude which St. Ignatius refers to in
The Spiritual Exercises is another aspect of
composition, the opening movement of the meditative
structure. As recommended by St. Ignatius, "The second
prelude is to ask God our Lord for what I want and
desire. The request must be according to the subject
matter."[6] Section 2 of "The Long Alley" contains the
protagonist's request, but in his own form and
language, not the more disciplined Ignatian mode. He

begins by asking, "Lord, what do you require?" (as if
employing a preparatory prayer) and then calls out to
the "Luminous one":

Come to me, milk-nose. I need a loan of
the quick.

There's no joy in soft bones.
For whom were you made, sweetness I
cannot touch?

Look what the larks do.
Luminous one, shall we meet on the bosom
of God?

Return the gaze of a pond. (CP 59).

The heart of his request is the "need" for "a loan of
the quick"--the quickening of his spirit as well as the
body; an enlivening which will lead, finally, to unity
of self, a condition of simplicity. The son's ultimate
effort, as Roethke explains in the letters, is "to
reach, to apprehend the unnamed 'Luminous one'"
(SL 141). He seeks to recover sexual potency ("milk-
nose") and the "light within light," but it is unclear
at the end of the stanza whether they will "meet on the
bosom of God" and find a mirror for the inner eye, the
soul, or merely return a narcissistic gaze in the
pond. The most significant line, however, in Ignatian
terms, is "The soul resides in the horse barn." In his
discussion of composition of place, St. Ignatius
explains how the meditator can create an image of a
subject that is invisible:

In meditations on subject matter that is
not visible, as here in meditation on
sins, the mental image will consist of
imagining, and considering my soul
imprisoned in its corruptible body, and
my entire being in this vale of tears as

an exile among brute beasts. By entire
being I mean body and soul.[7]

Though Roethke's use of the prelude is different, the
purpose is the same. Appropriately, the poet separates
rather than unifies body and soul, for the mental image
must   depend   upon   the   subject   matter   of   the
meditation. The son feels cut off from the "light" and
God in a state of sin and guilt and, therefore, "The
soul resides in the horse barn." As Roethke comments
in this letter to Babette Deutsch, the light achieved
by the son has given way to "a sense of unworthiness; a
vague sexual guilt" (SL 141).

The poem ends with an exertion of will and a
moment of acceptance. His statement "See what the will
wants" produces a minor ecstasy in which he seems to
grasp the significance of the natural world. Calling
on the flowers to "Come, come out of the shade, the
cool ways, / The long alleys of string and stem," he
feels the intense presence of "Light airs!" and the
"pierce of angels." He is enveloped by "tendrils";
"the leaves become me!" he exclaims (CP 61). Having
willed this sense of identity with nature, he is
prepared to deliver what Roethke calls "an exhortation
to the self: a demand for release and acceptance of
'The Fire'" (SL 141-42). "Give me my hands," he says,
"I'll take the fire," as if sexual guilt is shed and he
is ready to unite body and soul, the material and the
spiritual (CP 61).

In terms of the whole sequence, "The Lost Son" and
"The Long Alley" represent the stages of waiting and
acceptance preparatory to the phases of spiritual
growth which occur later in the son's journey.
Structurally, they function as composition, preludes
which create the son's mental and spiritual condition,

establish the nature of his search, and suggest the possibility that the light will return. The three poems that follow--"A Field of Light," "The Shape of the Fire," and "Praise to the End"--present the son's self-analysis. They evolve gradually through heightened states of awareness, culminating in the turning point of the sequence when the son gains an understanding of the self in relation to the light. In the final colloquies of the sequence--"Unfold! Unfold!", "I Cry, Love! Love!" and "O, Thou Opening, O"--the son experiences spiritual renewal and grows in understanding, learning that he can "Be a body lighted with love" and "can leap, true to the field": he does not need to reject the body in order to open himself to the life of the spirit (CP 98). The son continues to rock backward and forward between darkness and light until the field becomes "a soul's crossing time" (CP 89) and he feels himself to be "king of another condition" (CP 99).

"The Lost Son" concluded with the son experiencing the light on the frozen field "not alone," but at the beginning of "A Field of Light" he is once more immersed in a purgatorial world. He has come "to dead water, / Ponds with moss and leaves floating": "I was there alone / In a watery drowse" (CP 62). The three analytical discourses in this movement of the meditation represent the son's effort to achieve a new understanding of his condition and to recover the light. Roethke employs different methods of analysis in each poem, modes by which the son struggles out of the "mire," the "Void." In "A Field of Light" the son begins by asking the "Angel within" if he "ever curse[d] the sun," requesting the spirit to "Speak and abide" (CP 62). This petition is followed by two

rituals performed "at the edge of field," indicative of
the son's estrangement from the source of light and the
center of the soul. The boy searches for the "hidden"
"Under the blackened leaves," "In the deep grass" and
"Along the low ground dry only in August" (CP 62).
Then "Alone, I kissed the skin of a stone; / Marrow-
soft, danced in the sand" (CP 63). The act of kissing
the stone, "an absolute mode of being,"[8] precipitates
a heightened consciousness in which the son sees "The
lovely diminutives" and seems to experience his own
being through elemental nature:

> I could watch! I could watch!
> I saw the separateness of all things!
> My heart lifted up with great grasses;
> The weeds believed me, and the nesting
>   birds.
> . . . .
> And I walked, I walked through the light
>   air;
> I moved with the morning. (CP 63).

Seeing "the separateness of all things!" is a state of
awareness which precedes what Rudolf Otto, in Mysticism
East and West, calls the "lowest stage" of the "vision
of unity." In his discussion of the soul's perception
of the unity of all things Otto quotes this passage
from Meister Eckhart:

> Say, Lord, when is a man in mere
> "understanding" (in discursive
> intellectual understanding). I say to
> you: "When a man sees one thing
> separated from another." And when is a
> man above mere understanding? That I
> can tell you: "When he sees all in all,

    then   a   man   stands   beyond   mere
    understanding."[9]
During   this   phase   of   Roethke's   poetry,   the
protagonist's   intellectual   understanding   is   below   the
perception   of   all   created   things   as   one,   reflected   in
and   emanating   from   Divine   Reality.

        The   increased   activity   at   the   end   of   the   poem
enlivens   the   son   to   continue   self-analysis   in   "The
Shape   of   the   Fire":   "Is   he   a   bird   or   a   tree?"   "What
more   will   the   bones   allow?"   (CP   64).   Knowing   that
"This   is   only   the   edge   of   whiteness,"   the   initial
quickening   of   the   soul,   he   calls   the   spirit   to   aid   him
in   his   journey: "Spirit,   come   near"   (CP   64).   The   son
still   hangs   between   multiplicity   and   simplicity,   not
knowing   what   more   the   bones   will   permit.   Soon   it   is
"Time   for   the   flat-headed   man,"   the   "listener"   he
recognizes   as   "Him   with   the   platitudes   and   rubber
doughnuts,"   perhaps   his   conscience,   the   working   of   God
in   the   inner   self,   and   asks: "Have   you   come   to   unhinge
my   shadow?"   (CP   65).   Until   the   soul   is   liberated   he
will   continue   to   feel   that   the   body   is   devouring   him--
"My   meat   eats   me"--and   will   wonder   "Who   waits   at   the
gate?"   (CP   65).   "Renew   the   light,"   he   cries   to   the
"lewd   whisper"   (CP   65).

        This   plea   precipitates   a   key   moment   in   the   son's
discourse,   the   new   level   of   understanding   expressed   in
Section   3   of   the   poem:

    The wasp waits,
        The edge cannot eat the center.
    The grape glistens.
        The   path   tells   little   to   the
        serpent.
    An eye comes out of the wave.
        The journey from flesh is longest.

> A rose sways least.
>   The redeemer comes a dark way. (CP 66).

The son is still on the long "journey from flesh,"
acting out what Roethke poses in a 1946 notebook: "Are
we closest to knowledge when we are farthest from the
body?" (6 #83).   He takes the first step toward
knowledge, however, when he recognizes that the body's
fear and hatred of the soul or spirit is irrational,
for "The edge cannot eat the center." The soul, the
center of the self, will survive after being freed,
"unhinged". The son knows that "A rose sways least,"
but he is still seeking through the darkness to reach
this stillness-in-motion, a mystical condition in which
the self will achieve pure simplicity. The eye in the
wave which had "tilted" in the "dead water" of "A Field
of Light" will be the "Eye" asking him to "Come" to a
new sense of inner harmony at the end of the meditative
sequence (CP 99).

Before the son can reach this creative order, and
thus be wholly born, the imagination assists him in
journeying "further back" before he was born when
"Death was not": "Rain sweetened the cave and the dove
still called" (CP 66). This memory of a time when the
spirit still called and "love sang toward" produces a
new state of clarity. Roethke's use of infinities
establishes the son's conditon. They are embodiments
of his knowledge, suggesting fulfilled action. The
protagonist, now "the mature man," fully apprehends the
processes of nature as symbolic (SL 142):

> To have the whole air!--
>
> . . . .
>
> To be by the rose
> Rising slowly out of its bed,

Still as a child in its first
    loneliness;
. . . . . .
To know that light falls and fills,
    often without our knowing,
As an opaque vase fills to the brim from
    a quick pouring,
Fills and trembles at the edge yet does
    not flow over,
Still holding and feeding the stem of
    the contained flower

(CP 67).

In "A Field of Light" the son's experience of heightened vitality, his feeling of being extended "through the light air," is produced, as Roethke puts it, by "intensity in the seeing" (SP 25). That same intensity causes him to discover in the unfolding rose that "The light, the full sun" generates and sustains an ordered world (CP 67).

"Praise to the End!" is the title poem of the volume in which Roethke published the entire Lost Son Sequence for the first time in 1951. In the letters he describes the sequence as "a kind of tensed-up Prelude" (SL 148), and it is clear from the following lines that the title of this final analytical discourse is borrowed from Wordsworth's Prelude, the subtitle of which is "The Growth of a Poet's Mind, An Autobiographical Poem."

Dust as we are, the immortal spirit
    grows
Like harmony in music; there is a dark
Inscrutable workmanship that reconciles
Discordant elements, makes them cling
    together

In one society. How strange, that all
The terrors, pains, and early miseries,
Regrets, vexations, lassitudes
   interfused
Within my mind, should e'er have borne a
   part,
And that a needful part, in making up
The calm existence that is mine when I
Am worthy of myself! Praise to the
   end![10]

At this stage in his growth the lost son is unable to
reconcile the "Discordant elements" to form a "calm
existence." He still feels unworthy of such
simplicity, for he remains in the Dantean dark wood
where there is no intuition of the eternal: "The rings
have gone from the pond, / the river's alone with its
water" (CP 85). Sexual and spiritual images merge as
he expresses his impotence ("All risings / Fall") and
addresses first his body ("soft mocker") then "My
dearest dust," calling out to "frosty beard"--"Speak to
me" (CP 85-86). The understanding he reaches
represents the first movement of the inner will, a
motion which prepares for the colloquies in which
wisdom is achieved: "I conclude! I conclude! / My
dearest dust, I can't stay here" (CP 86). He must
journey beyond the purgatorial wood and the "bower of
dead skin" for "This salt can't warm a stone"
(CP 86). The way out of the darkness toward the
quickening of the spirit is by sharp stones with the
wind at his back, through the ebb and flow of memory
and dream when "Desire was winter-calm" (CP 87). His
ultimate questions--"Is the eternal near," "Can the
bones breathe?--and the final plea, "Ghost, come
closer," lead him to the moment when he is "awake all

over" (CP 87-88). Having "crawled from the mire," he knows "the stone's eternal pulseless longing" to be his own yearning for the eternal (CP 88).

The final section of "Praise to the End!" is difficult to interpret as part of the son's spiritual growth, for Roethke comments in "Open Letter" that the poem ends with a euphoric passage which resolves into an onanistic death-wish (SP 40). Though the language of the passage lends itself to this analysis, it also accommodates another interpretation. The passage can be viewed as a moment when the protagonist renews the experience of having shared his identity with the subhuman--"Many astounds before, I lost my identity to a pebble"--and now "bask[s] in the bower of change" (CP 88). "I believe!" he exclaims, "In the winter-wasp, pulsing its wings in the sunlight" (CP 88). The ecstasy expressed demonstrates the extent to which the self has penetrated the natural world. "The protagonist, for all his joy, is still 'alone,'" Roethke states (SP 40). Even though he is separated from other human beings and God, he has experienced the "otherness" of natural creatures, possibly a necessary step toward subsequent unions. It is true that the dark once beguiled him, for "I remember the sea-faced uncles," he says. The important question for this study, however, is whether he is still being drawn back to the dark water or toward spiritual awakening. A consideration of the last stanza is crucial to an understanding of the protagonist's growth:

> Wherefore, O birds and small fish,
>   surround.
> Lave me, ultimate waters.
> The dark showed me a face.

My ghosts are all gay.
The light becomes me
                    (CP 88).
Roethke stresses that the poem is only "a dead-end
explored," and that "In terms of the whole sequence,
[the hero] survives. . . . His self-consciousness, his
very will to live saves him from the 'annihilation' of
the ecstasy" (SP 40). The explanation emphasizes the
coherence of the sequence but mutes a possible meaning
of the final lines. In my view, the death-wish--"Lave
me, ultimate waters"--may also function as purgation, a
cleansing by eternal waters. Moveover, a
transformation occurs in the last line: "The light
becomes me," the protagonist proclaims. This
affirmation, with its suggestion that the hero feels
the presence of the light within the self, seems to
indicate that the lost son is beginning to accept the
light of the soul even as he earlier accepted the fire
of the body.

The colloquies that follow this turning point are
understood by St. Francis de Sales and St. Ignatius to
be the result of the analytical discourses during
meditation. That is, meditation moves the will to
speak to Christ from the heart, as one would engage in
a conversation with a friend, and to make practical
resolutions concerning the subject of meditation. St.
Francis expands the possibilities of address to include
the self, saints, angels, or even inanimate
creatures. He also states that as a natural outcome of
analysis the self may be awakened "to a sense of
compassion, wonder and joy."[11]

The colloquies of Roethke's protagonist employ
forms of address and methods of development appropriate
to the meditative subject, the son's anguish concerning

the relationship between the life of the body and the growth of the spirit. Until this moment his separation from the father (God) and his sense of sexual guilt have hindered him from participating in the life of the spirit and achieving wholeness, the condition of simplicity. Having touched the creative order of existence and learned that "Light becomes me," the son is ready to be assisted by the soul's powers in attaining a new state of being. The terms of address vary with each poem, but in each instance he converses with a part of himself, whether his bones, his conscience, or the inner self. Ultimately, the colloquies demonstrate the protagonist's will to resolve his inner conflict. Actions essential to his progress are indicated by the titles of the poems. First he sees with the inner eye and "unfolds" toward the invisible as "The bulb unravels" toward the sun (CP 90). Having apprehended the value of the intuitive vision, he rejects the aid of reason and announces that he has reached "a condition of joy" (CP 92). Finally, he recognizes that "I'm lost in what I have"--that what grace the body has is not enough--and "opens" himself to the light of the soul (CP 97). During his colloquies Roethke's hero is aided not by the will alone but by memory and understanding as well. Memories of earlier experiences combined with the actions of the will and a heightened consciousness resulting from the colloquies lead him finally to a new existence.

"Unfold! Unfold!" opens with the son telling the "spirit" that he has come "By snails, by leaps of frog" to this point in his journey (CP 89). He has often called on the snails to be "near," to assist him in his progress; moreover, as we will see at the end of the

sequence, his inward turning toward the depths of the
self and his search for the soul have reflected the
snail's design. Speaking to his "body without skin,"
the son explains that he "Can't crawl back through
those veins" again, down into the unconscious in search
of revelation. "I ache for another choice," he says
(CP 89). When "Eternity howls in the last crags" he
must make a choice and find another way (CP 89).
Suddenly he recognizes that the frozen field where he
had first seen the possibility of "light within light"
has become "a soul's crossing time" (CP 89). "No
longer simple," the field may create the son's passage
to spiritual renewal, even if he must leap alone in
seeking a new perception.

The speakers who establish this rite of passage
are "Mr. Pinch" and "a dead tongue" that says "halloo"
(CP 89-90). Mr. Pinch pronounces a "whelm of proverbs"
as a parent would to a child, but his words cause the
son to remember going "far back" into the unconscious
where he "nearly whispered [himself] away" (CP 89).
This memory of the journey back to the moment of birth
makes him realize how "Easy the life of the mouth" was
before he experienced guilt, fear and death (CP 90).
Associating the mouth with various creative openings,
he suddenly feels a rising motion--"Who's floating?
Not me"--and attains a new level of understanding:
"The eye perishes in the small vision" (CP 90). To
look only at the visible, whether the physical self or
created nature, destroys the inner self or soul and
denies the world of the spirit. Hearing the "dead
tongue" of his father speak encourages the son and

precipitates his discovery that "All simple creatures" are "symbols" that sing of an unseen reality (CP 90).

Roethke borrowed the title "Unfold! Unfold!" from Henry Vaughan's poem, "the Revival":

Unfold, unfold! take in His light,
Who makes thy Cares more short than
    night.[12]

The last lines of the poem, quoted in a 1948 notebook, are especially revealing, I think:

And here in dust and dirt, O here
The Lilies of His love appear! (7 #100).

Like Vaughan, Roethke considers the natural world "a field for revelation":

Speak to the stones, and the stars
    answer.
At first the visible obscures:
Go where light is (CP 90).

Roethke comments upon the "reality of the unseen" in a 1946-48 notebook entry: "there is an unseen order and our supreme good lies in adjusting ourselves to it" (8 #112). If such an adjustment is to take place he must "Go where Light is" because "The eye perishes in the small vision" (CP 90). "The eye, of course, is not enough," Roethke says; "but the outer eye serves the inner, that's the point" (6 #88). Discussing the "true archetype of the soul," Meister Eckhart wrote,

The soul has two eyes—one looking
inwards and the other outwards. It is
the inner eye of the soul that looks
into essence and takes being directly
from God. That is its true function.
The soul's outward eye is directed
toward creatures and perceives their
external forms but when a person turns

inwards and knows God in terms of his
own awareness of him, in the roots of
his being, he is then freed from all
creation and is secure in the castle of
truth.[13]

In Eckhart's terms, Roethke uses the soul's outer eye
to experience a sense of cosmic unity, thereby creating
the felt apprehensions of the poetry: "Speak to the
stones, and the stars answer" (CP 90). It is this
intuitive vision that brings forth the "shy ecstasies
of half knowledge" which Roethke mentions in a 1948-49
notebook (7 #267).

The son wonders if he has heard his father's
voice--a call from beyond the grave to guide him--but
this half knowledge does not cause him to alter the
pace or the direction of his journey out of the mire:

I'll seek my own meekness.
What grace I have is enough.
The lost have their own pace
(CP 91).

The child who defined himself as "crazed and graceless"
now seems convinced that what grace the body has
achieved is sufficient. He admits that the thrashing
of the dead has helped, but "What the grave says, / The
nest denies" (CP 91). The nest insists that birth is
the only creative opening and thus it alone should be
praised. Believing that it is enough to "seek [his]
own meekness" the son languishes. Other speakers must
pursuade before his confusion and anguish will subside.

"Delight me otherly, white spirit," the son pleads
at the beginning of "I Cry, Love! Love!" (CP 92).
Though he desires another condition, he wants to remain
in the natural world. "Is circularity such a shame?"
he asks (CP 92). Would it be such a shame to circulate

into the invisible, returning with the news, the secret
of eternal life? The correspondences which he embraced
in the previous poem were part of a vision which has
now receded. Fear has returned. "What else can
befall?" he asks his "little bones" (CP 92). Seeking
his own mode of knowing, he belittles reason, calling
it "That dreary shed, that hutch for grubby
schoolboys!" (CP 92). Reason is the halfway house of
fear, not the "field for revelation." He listens to
the song of the hedgewren telling him of a simplicity
known by the child which the man can recover through
"That anguish of concreteness!"--the singing
abstractions of the natural world. By observing and
participating in natural processes he can "proclaim
once more a condition of joy" (CP 92). Hearing the
"dry cry" from his inner "desert" reinforces the fact
that "The bones are lonely"; "Beginnings start without
shade," he says, suggesting that the spirit is
acquired, not born within us. Not until he sees "the
face of the lake" tilt "backward and forward" as the
"water recedes" in a "rocking" motion does he remember
the one he "met in a nest" before he was born (CP
93). This memory of the source of life, of the one
"Who untied the tree," leads him to grasp the knowledge
that "We never enter / Alone" (CP 93). Thus the poem
ends with a reassuring image, an intuition of the birth
of the soul with the body and the possibility that the
mature man can embrace this union.

The determination to "make it; but it may take me"
is the cry of the protagonist's will as the final
colloquy begins (CP 97). He calls to the "dizzy
aphorist" to "Dazzle" him with a "precept," for "I'm
lost in what I have," he says (CP 97). It is this
knowledge, a reverse echo of "What grace I have is

enough," which motivates him to become "simplicity's
sweet thing" (CP 98). He is also aided by an image of
his "father's face" seen "deep in the belly of a thing
to be," suggesting that rebirth is possible (CP 97).
The turning point comes, however, in his dialogue with
the inner self in Section 2 of the poem. The son
addresses the self in prose, calling it "Bag-Foot," as
if it is a bag of wind and a foot that must be
wrestled. In a tone of disgust he attacks the self,
telling it he isn't interested in having "that
pelludious Jesus-shimmer over all things"--"light's
broken speech revived" (CP 98). Speaking in anguish
the next moment, he goads the self--"Who ever said God
sang in your fat shape?"--reminding it that "A leaf
could drag you": it is not a fine example of sturdy
simplicity (CP 98).

The "inner I" responds in verse, persuading the
son slowly concerning what it means to be. The central
lesson is that "The dark has its own light. / A son has
many fathers" (CP 98). He must say "Yes" to the whole
of existence, embracing the darkness as well as the
light, acknowledging all the sources of life. This
recognition--"You mean?-- / I can leap, true to the
field" and "Be a body lighted with love"--makes the son
"wild with news!" (CP 98-99). He becomes a "webby
wonder," swaying "like a sapling tree" (CP 98). The
revitalization of the spirit is evident when he
exclaims, "My fancy's white!" (CP 99). When the inner
"Eye" says "Come," the son expresses the union of body
and soul: "This flesh has airy bones" (CP 99).

The protagonist's colloquy--"O, Thou Opening, O"--
concludes with a terse, dramatic comment on the nature
of the journey:

Going is knowing.
I see; I seek;
I'm near.
Be true,
Skin. (CP 99)

"I learn by going where I have to go," Roethke says in
"The Waking" (CP 108). In a notebook entry dated 1949
he comments that "The directionless learn only by going
(moving)" (8, #106), suggesting that the "knowing" is
found or created in the process--the very motion
itself--of seeing and seeking. The movement of the
mind backwards and forwards and the rocking motion on
the face of the lake have brought him closer to a
greater reality. Memory, intuitive understanding and
the colloquies have helped, but the journey has not
ended. "I'm near," he says.

The understanding of the motion of the spirit
which the protagonist is seeking is expressed in "A
Light Breather," Roethke's epilogue to the sequence.
It describes, metaphorically, the knowledge that "the
spirit need not be spare: it can grow gracefully and
beautifully like a tendril, like a flower" (SP 21).

The spirit moves,
Yet stays:
Stirs as a blossom stirs,
Still wet from its bud-sheath,
Slowly unfolding,
Turning in the light with its tendrils;
Plays as a minnow plays,
Tethered to a limp weed, swinging,
Tail around, nosing in and out of
   the current,
Its shadows loose, a watery finger;
Moves, like the snail,

> Still inward,
>
> Taking and embracing its surroundings,
>
> Never wishing itself away,
>
> Unafraid of what it is,
>
> A music in a hood,
>
> A small thing,
>
> Singing. (CP 101)

The sequence resolves, then, in the paradoxical motion of the spirit that moves, yet stays, a celebration of the soul unfolding and then turning inward. This knowledge is the result of the interpenetration of the self in touch with the creative source of life. The self sings, "Unafraid of what it is."

These poems contain the roots of the mystical view of reality found in Roethke's poetry, the first hints and half-guesses of a "reality more than the immediate" (SP 19): "Was it light within light? / Stillness becoming alive, / Yet still?" (CP 58); the perception of the natural world as symbolic: "a field for revelation" (CP 90); and the primacy of felt experience: "We think by feeling," Roethke says in "The Waking"; "What is there to know?" (CP 108). The lost son's spiritual awareness is a prelude to the Awakening and Illumination of the Self experienced by protagonists in later sequences. Recollection and the meditative process have been initiated, but the spiritual journey must be renewed before the phases of contemplation are attained. The Lost Son Sequence also embodies the first stage in the process of expansion during which a person transcends the phenomenal self, the ego, by "realizing new correspondences, new sympathies and affinities with the not-ourselves."[14] The lost son initiates this process by apprehending his own being in relation to "the lovely diminutives"

(<u>CP</u> 63), the animate and inanimate elements of the natural world.

In a 1948 notebook Roethke comments, "Part of me longs to circulate into the invisible" (10 #135). The key word, of course, is "circulate," a motion which only part of the self wished to engender. What he discloses in the poetry is that paradoxical sense of having gone and stayed: (The spirit moves, / Yet stays" (<u>CP</u> 101). To "circulate into the invisible" may mean to transcend the sense-world and glimpse eternity, returning to the "real" world a new man. More often, Roethke's speakers transform or re-create the self by contemplating the sense-world, apprehending the creative source of life through the symbols in the natural world. The longing for spiritual renewal expressed by the lost son and the protagonist of the "Sequence, Sometimes Metaphysical"--"to be something else, yet still to be" (<u>CP</u> 244)--is the force which activates Roethke's meditative sequences.

III

"MEDITATIONS OF AN OLD WOMAN"

"I would stretch in both directions, like the
root and branch of a tree."
                    --Roethke Notebooks (10 #135)

"Meditations of an Old Woman" is a "Journey within
a journey," another backward and forward motion typical
of spiritual progress (CP 158).   It illustrates the
awakening and release of the transcendent self as the
old woman meditates on the meaning of existence,
particularly whether the spirit continues after the
body dies. This movement parallels the rekindling of
the old woman's spirit and her ultimate release from
"the dreary dance of opposites" (CP 178)--"the cold
fleshless kiss of contraries" (CP 166). The poems in
the sequence oscillate between aridity and joy, periods
of repose and activity, as if the soul is waiting to
gather itself together, to energize its powers, before
it rises again, increasing its activity. Its affective
power grows throughout the sequence, corresponding to
the animation of the spirit in the field, both the
"field for revelation" and the field of consciousness.
     At the end of "First Meditation" a "flame,
intense, visible, / . . . / moves over the field, /
Without burning," suggesting the possibility of
spiritual renewal. The seed of the soul is present but
its energy is dormant. In "I'm Here" the old woman
speaks bravely to "the wind" of eternity as if invoking
the Eternal Spirit. Reality comes closer in "Her
Becoming" as she hears a voice in her sleep--"Dare I
embrace a ghost from my own breast?"--and sees the
spirit-child run ahead of her (CP 165). By releasing
this eternal friend, the old woman "become[s] the
wind," embracing air, light and stones. The release of

the spirit is depicted as she tells the birds "My
breath is more than yours," becoming "A rapt thing with
a name" (CP 167). The field where the flame first
appeared is now her friend, she says, "the long light"
her "home" (CP 167). "I hum in pure vibration, like a
saw," she proclaims, describing her new inner melody.
In "Fourth Meditation" she and the soul wait at the
edge of the field for the pure moment, "Seeking in
[her] own way, eternal purpose" (CP 168). This
attitude of reverent anticipation, as if holding new
beginnings within her changing body, causes her to
think of herself in terms of the breath she breathes:
"I breathe what I am: The first and last of all
things" (CP 170). When the eternal child breaks
through the barrier of fear, moving from the sub- or
pre-conscious world of sleep into the field of
consciousness, "long looking" is intensified and the
will is moved. The old woman seeks her own "meekness"
or humility, recovering a "tenderness" for all living
things. Soon she "lives in light's extreme,"
stretching "in all directions," feeling that she has
"gone and stayed" (CP 173). She stands in the midst of
light, knowing that "Existence dares perpetuate a soul"
(CP 173). Now that the self has been illuminated by
the spirit it can journey forth in the "North American
Sequence" to experience the elemental opposites and
establish the unified self in the natural world. The
poetic knowledge grasped by Roethke during the writing
of the old woman's meditations prepares him, then, to
undertake a further exploration of the relationship of
self, soul and nature.

This description of the rebirth and subsequent
activity of the spirit follows Jacques Maritain's
analysis of the work of inspiration in generating

poetic intuition. Inspiration influences the creation
of poetic intuition in the seat of the soul,
functioning in two phases. The poet begins by
returning to the source of creativity, the hidden spot
at the center of the soul where all the soul's powers
are gathered in unity. The means by which he enters
this deep place is "a recollection, fleeting as it may
be, of all the senses, and a kind of unifying repose
which is like a natural grace, a primordial gift."[1]
The first phase of inspiration, then, is "the phase of
systole and unifying repose."[2] Through concentration
and meditation the poet penetrates the forces gathered
in the soul. That is, he emulates the repose of the
soul's powers in order to reach this "natural grace."

A comment Roethke made in a 1959-60 notebook
indicates that he was aware of the grace necessary for
poetic creativity: "Difficult, hard writing requires
not a graceful mind but a mind of grace--an altogether
different and higher thing" (13 #188). What is needed
is that blessed tranquility which is above the
effortless skill of the mind. A mind of grace is in
touch with the soul's natural grace, the genesis of
creative intuition. The poet meets the Muse, as
Maritain states, "within the soul," for it is an
intuition that comes to him "from above conceptual
reason" [his italics].[3] Beginning with the germ of a
poem, the poet initiates the first phase of inspiration
by recollecting all the senses in quiet concentration
and gradually awakening their vitality or "dormant
energy."[4] After this gathering of the soul's powers
the breath of inspiration rises and the poet seems to
expand. This rising coincides with the movement of
poetic intuition from the preconscious to the conscious
life of the mind; that is, the soul's powers, no longer

dormant, become agents activating poetic intuition. When inspiration rises it enters the second "phase of diastole," activity which "manifests itself either negatively, by a breaking of barriers, or positively, by the entrance of poetic intuition into the field of consciousness."[5] The creative motion of this second phase is the activity usually referred to as inspiration. The two phases may be distinguished by considering the difference between "inspiration in its primary seed or as poetic intuition and inspiration as all-pervading motion."[6]

The movement of the old woman's spirit toward illumination corresponds to the phases by which creative intuition is generated in the poet's soul. In the opening lyrics the seed of illumination is visible, but the energy of the soul is dormant. She gathers herself in recollection, journeying backward in time in the hope of finding a clue to the meaning of her existence so that the spirit will desire to continue. The invocation of the Spirit at the end of "I'm Here," defiant and tough though it may be, seems to prepare for the beginning of the second phase, the release of the breath of inspiration in the form of the eternal child. This movement or catalytic force causes an expansion of the self wherein she apprehends nature as symbolic and becomes a vibrant soul. Following a period of waiting and self-analysis she expands further, reaching out to the "self-involved" and gathering the extremes of birth and death into the self. This quiet activity grounds the soul for the all-pervading motion of inspiration which occurs in the final lyric, "What Can I Tell My Bones?" During the height of this second phase the old woman experiences self-illumination through natural contemplation or

"long looking" and is released from her anxiety by a
spirit outside herself. The meditative activity at the
end of the sequence is the work of poetic intuition, a
spiritual agent at the root of the soul, one which
possesses the soul's natural grace and is thereby in
touch with the Eternal Spirit.

The old woman's progress toward illumination is
depicted in the form of an interior drama which follows
the meditative structure of composition, analysis and
colloquy. The five poems of the sequence are a
meditation on the old woman's spiritual condition as
she approaches death, an exploration of the spirit's
effort to continue. Employing memory, understanding
and will, the old woman gathers or pieces together not
only the self but also the meaning of existence.
Roethke wrote in "On Identity'": "The human problem
is to find out what one really is: whether one exists,
whether existence is possible. But How? 'Am I but
nothing, leaning toward a thing?'" (SP 20). To
discover this meaning, Roethke's lady "stretch[es] in
both directions, like the root and branch of a tree"
(10 #135). Though there is no evidence that this 1948
notebook entry refers to the old woman, the stretching
it describes speaks of her movement toward the stones
and the wind--all part of her effort to seek news of
the eternal life of the spirit. Both elements are
symbols of absolute modes of being which aid the old
woman in embracing beginnings and endings within
herself. The path that her journey follows is an
existential rendering of the initial steps of the
Mystic Way: Awakening, Purification, and Illumination
of the Self. Her interior monologue begins in
questioning and self-searching but stretches toward
humility, an attitude which prepares her to receive the

answer to the problem of her meditation. At the end of her explorations, the old woman has resolved her inner conflicts, becoming one with herself and with created nature. Instead of realizing Union with the Absolute, she experiences a sense of rebirth, the joyous fulfillment of the first two Degrees of Interior Prayer, Recollection and Quiet. The senses and all visible things aid in producing a condition of mind or spirit through which she can receive the final message.

Roethke's lady--"that old woman upon whom life is settling down" (5 #64)--is a tough lady who is seeking spiritual renewal. The poet began "Meditations of an Old Woman" in 1955 shortly after the death of his mother. In his comments on Words for the Wind, the volume in which the sequence was published in 1958, Roethke explained that "The protagonist was modelled, in part, after [his] mother . . . whose favorite reading was the Bible, Jane Austen, and Dostoyevsky--in other words, a gentle, highly articulate old lady believing in the glories of the world, yet fully conscious of its evils" (SP 58). Later, in a letter to Ralph J. Mills, Jr., the poet comments further upon the nature of the old woman in an effort to counteract suggestions that parts of the sequence "seemed to contain parodies of Eliot":

> As for the old lady poems, I wanted (1) to create a character for whom such [Whitmanesque meditative] rhythms are indigenous; that she be a dramatic character, not just me. Christ, Eliot in the Quartets is tired, spiritually tired, old-man. Rhythm, Tiresome Tom. Is my old lady tired? The hell she is: she's tough, she's brave, she's aware of life and she would take

a congeries of eels over a hassle of bishops
    any day (SL 231).
This brave old lady who is "aware of life" struggles
toward Illumination of the Self by confronting her
anxiety over non-being. Since Roethke believes that
the "struggle for spiritual identity" is a "perpetual
recurrence," many of the insights gained by the lost
son are renewed by the old woman (SP 41). "Spiritual
growth's an oscillatory thing," he comments in a
1949-50 notebook: "we move by shivers in the world's
tumultuous spine" (8 #113). These poems, like the Lost
Son Sequence, are dominated by a pattern of recurring
cycles of darkness and light. Ultimately, however, her
clarity of vision is marked by a mystical intuition
impossible for the son to achieve. The answer to "What
can I tell my bones?" comes suddenly, almost
unexpectedly, after she has worked through her anxiety
by using the powers or agents of the soul: memory,
understanding and will (CP 172).

      In the opening poem of the sequence, "First
Meditation," Roethke presents a concrete description of
a bleak landscape, a vivid portrayal of the old womn's
spiritual condition. St. Ignatius suggests that the
devotional meditation should begin with a prelude which
he calls "composition of place, seeing the spot," a
practice which Roethke employs in poetic rather than
devotional terms.[7] The mental process is the same,
however: the imagination is used to create a setting
in which the thing to be contemplated may be found.
The old woman's physical and mental state as well as
the fact of death approaching are movingly represented
in the opening stanzas: "weeds hiss at the edge of the
field"; "stones loosen on the obscure hillside"; "a
tree tilts from its roots" (CP 157). She has become "a

strange piece of flesh, / Nervous and cold, bird-
furtive, whiskery," a woman who wonders, "How can I
rest in the days of my slowness?" (CP 157). Though
"the sun brings joy to some," "the rind, often, hates
the life within," knowing that it will eventually ripen
and culminate in decay. On this day--"love's worst
ugly day"--she is aware that "The spirit moves, but not
always upward" (CP 157).

The subject of the old woman's interior drama is
suggested by her question, "How can I rest in the days
of my slowness?" (CP 157). What knowledge will calm
her restless body, mind and spirit? From what source
will it come? The hints are found in "First
Meditation," a prelude to the colloquy in which she
clarifies the problem of her meditation and receives
the final answer. The movement of the spirit, she
says, is "not always upward." Instead, the spirit
"that tries for another life, / Another way and place
in which to continue" (CP 159), moves with the tentative, awkward motion of a crab, its "tail and smaller
legs slipping and sliding slowly backward" (CP 159).
The old woman also compares the journey of the spirit
to the movement of the tired salmon as it struggles
against "the rush of brownish-white water, / Still
swimming forward" (CP 159). Both of these images
illustrate the slow progress implied in Roethke's
statement that "to go forward as a spiritual man it is
necessary first to go back" (SP 39). The entire
meditative sequence represents the journey of the old
woman as she seeks another life and finds a way to
continue living in the face of death.

At first she "seems" to go "Backward in time,"
recalling a childhood memory of two sparrows singing
antiphonally, one perched on an air vent inside a

greenhouse, the other "outside, in the bright day, /
With a wind from the west and the trees all in motion"
(CP 158). These birds, their "songs tumbling over and
under the glass," represent, metaphorically, the ideal
spiritual condition: "Both inner and outer reality the
same: the final secret" (8 #112). The remembered
happiness of this moment in the greenhouse does not
bring relief to her barren existence, however. The
revelation she searches for in "the waste lonely places
/ Behind the eye" is not found: "There is no riven
tree, or lamb dropped by an eagle" (CP 159). There are
only signs of mortality: "the motes of dust in the
immaculate hallways, / The darkness of falling hair,
the warnings from lint and spiders" (CP 159). But
"There are still times," she says, "morning and
evening," when the revelation seems to be waiting
expectantly (CP 159). These moments of stillness-in-
motion occur within the natural world yet are not subject to the flow of time.

> A fume reminds me, drifting across wet
>   gravel;
> A cold wind comes over stones;
> A flame, intense, visible,
> Plays over the dry pods,
> Runs fitfully along the stubble,
> Moves over the field,
> Without burning.
>   In such times, lacking a god,
>   I am still happy (CP 160).

This flame that moves without burning and the happiness
that it produces are the first signs of the spiritual
awakening which the old woman will experience later in
the meditation. The potentiality for mystical
experience is present in this image, but it cannot be

realized until the old woman has continued her journey backward and is psychologically ready to receive the insight which will provide spiritual stability.

"I'm Here," the next poem in the sequence, appears to be a second prelude, another stage which prepares for the main points of the meditation, yet it also contains elements of analysis. "Dare I shrink to a hag?" she asks. Memory and the senses assist her in this phase of her journey. Having established the setting and the subject of her meditation, the old woman journeys backward in time, recalling threshold experiences of her youth, images of "ill-defined dying," those times of growth which have brought her to "another place and time, / Another condition: (CP 162). Though she is "tired of tiny noises" and "The prattle of the young no longer pleases," she remembers when she was once "queen of the vale," delighting in running through all grass, responding intensely to life with her senses, "pleased to be" (CP 161-62). In Section 3 of the poem she recalls several half-understood, seemingly irrational moments when she experienced feelings and images from a level deeper than ordinary consciousness: the scent of half-opened rose buds which almost smothered her when she bent down to untangle her dress; the image of something fluttering on the sill of the eye when she slowly came out of sleep; the sight of "small figures dancing, / A congress of tree-shrews and rats, / Romping around a fire" when she closed her eyes during an illness (CP 163). After these reflections, the old woman turns to the present, to the time when she, like her geranium, is dying, "for all I can do, / Still leaning toward the last place the sun was" (CP 163). Instead of enjoying sensual pleasures, as she did in her youth,

she "wears" roses by "looking away." She rejoices not
only in "the act of seeing" but also in "the fresh
after-image" which exists "Without commotion."   "I
prefer the still joy," she says: "A snail's music"
(CP 163).   In the final section of the poem the old
woman makes a bold attempt to dismiss her fear of
death, rationalizing its finality: "Even carp die in
this river. / . . . / I've done all the singing I
would. / . . . / It's not my first dying" (CP 164).
Finally she addresses the wind as if it is the on-
coming force of eternity.   In words indicative of her
tough nature, she exclaims:

If the wind means me,

I'm here!

Here (CP 164).

The old woman does not persist in this attitude,
however.   In "Her Becoming," the analytical phase of
her meditation, her soul is aided by memory and the
intuitive   faculty   and   she   becomes   spiritually
renewed.   At this point in her spiritual drama the
journey backward has ended and she is ready to consider
"a jauntier principle of order" (CP 165) which will
lead her to the moment when she is able to "hum in
vibration, like a saw" (CP 167).   Roethke expresses her
need in a 1951 notebook: "I demand from you, deepest
self, some jaunty principle or order" (9 #119).   The
change which occurs in the old woman is initiated by
her momentary perception of a voice, "a low sweet
watery noise," that rises from the unconscious in her
early sleep:

Dare I embrace a ghost from my own breast?

A spirit plays before me like a child,

A child at play, a wind-excited bird (CP 165).

Through the image of child and bird the old woman touches the deepest region of the self, her buried spiritual life; yet she questions the existence of this "ghost from the soul's house": "Who knows / The way out of a rose?" (CP 165). Though she may dream of "a jauntier principle of order," she awakes to her "usual diet of shadows"; once again she knows "the cold flesh-less kiss of contraries, / The nerveless constriction of surfaces" (CP 165-166). Despite these shadows, the spirit has been awakened and the Self, the "inner I," begins to emerge.

Having stolen from sleep a glimpse of the eternal spirit, she takes from memory an experience which can only be termed mystical--a description of one of those times when "reality comes closer: / In a field, in the actual air" (CP 166). She remembers a time when the Self emerged and stood outside herself. The "inner I" ran ahead of her across a field, into a wood, and breathlessly listened to the stones until "All natural shapes became symbolical" (CP 166). As this statement from a 1945-46 notebook explains, "'Every visible and invisible creature is a theophany or appearance of God'--Erigena" (12 #174). This sudden and acute realization of "reality" causes her to shed her clothes and run again, crying her new life to the fox and the wren. Her vision expands until she declares, "I have seen! . . . The holy line! / A small place all in flame." She ends by approaching a state of pure being: "A rapt thing with a name" (CP 167).

This memory of the emergence of the transcendent self precipitates the old woman's experience of the first stage of mystical awareness: the moment of spiritual awakening. Underhill describes the awakening of the self as "a sudden, intense and joyous perception

of God immanent in the universe" (M 179). Its salient
characteristics   are   "a   sense   of   liberation   and
victory: a conviction of the nearness of God: a sen-
timent of love towards God" (M 179).   Although the old
woman does not mention God, the intensity of her voice
and the soaring motion of her rhythms vividly depict
the   knowledge   she   has   discovered   of   the   eternal
immanent in the natural world.   In the final section of
the poem she seems to become a pure spirit:

> A shape without a shade, or almost none,
> I hum in pure vibration, like a saw.
> The grandeur of a crazy one alone!-
> By swoops of bird, by leaps of fish, I live.
> My shadow steadies in a shifting stream;
> I live in air; the long light is my home;
> I dare caress the stones, the field my friend;
> A light wind rises: I become the wind
>
> (CP 167).

These   images   are   one   of   Roethke's   finest   representations of the liberating force of the spirit, a force
which creates the old woman's paradoxical condition of
stillness-in-motion / motion-in-stillness.   her shadow
"steadies" in the flux of the stream and she becomes
the wind whose "home is the long light."

The steadying of her spirit produces a state of
Interior   Quiet   in   which   the   old   woman   experiences
purification of the self.   "Fourth Meditation" depicts
her manner of seeking purgation, a way which involves
self-simplification but not in the usual form described
in mystical literature.   Roethke recorded Richard of
St. Victor's definition of purgation from Underhill's
study: "The   essence   of   purgation   is   self-
simplification"   (12   #27,   cf.   M   204).   Considered
broadly,   then,   purgation   entails   simplifying   the

interests and motives of the self and renouncing temporal existence as unreal (M 204). It is the slow, painful process of turning the self from the unreal toward the Absolute. Unlike the contemplative, however, Roethke's lady does not detach herself from all finite things; rather, she opens herself to the wisdom of natural objects and seeks "eternal purpose" by standing "At the edge of the field waiting for the pure moment" (CP 168). Her attitude of waiting, a state of mind receptive to final answers, is one of her modes of self-purification. But it is effortless, indicative of her belief that knowledge of the eternal comes suddenly. She does appear to have partially overcome the senses, however, for she recognizes that " . . . a time comes when the vague life of the mouth no longer suffices" (CP 168). She waits and looks for evidence of a deeper existence to which the soul can be grounded. Her way of simplifying the self is to be aware of her waiting soul, "lonely in its choice," and to listen to the noise of death in her body (CP 168).

As Underhill explains, however, true purgation is a painful undertaking which requires stripping the self of the "I," the ego, and then cleansing or remaking what remains so that the deeper center of the self may live. Thus the superficial self dies and the inner self prepares for Union with Divine Reality. One of the most orderly guides to the contemplative life, Augustine Baker (1575-1641), has clarified the nature of the purgative way. Baker's understanding of this process of self-mortification, quoted by Underhill, appears in Roethke's notebooks: "Mortification tends to subject the body to the spirit and the spirit to God" (15 #217; cf. M 218). The old woman's experience is entirely different, however; one which is indicative

of her inner self and her spiritual condition. Instead
of undergoing the agonizing task of abating self-love
and self-will, she participates in a moment of self-
definition, seeming to negate its importance, and then
she thinks of the "self-involved," wishing that they
may "flame into being!" (CP 169). These two acts are
her way of achieving self-mortification. She poses the
question, "What is it to be a woman?" but when the
answer is presented as a series of questions, it
suggests that self-identity is no longer of
significance. Having transcended selfhood, her vision
enlarges. Reaching beyond the uncertainties of her own
soul she wishes that "The ritualists of the mirror, the
lonely drinkers"--the "gentle and beautiful still-to-
be-born"--may be awakened to see "the sharp bones of
the poor," to know "the soul's authentic hunger" (CP
169). Ultimately, however, she returns to the agony of
her soul waiting in her changing body. Instead of
subjecting the body to the spirit and the spirit to
God, the old woman "sweats light from a stone" and
sings: "By singing we defend," she declares
(CP 170). Her meditation is her song--the spirit's way
of defending itself against the death of the body.

Self-purification prepares the old woman for the
moment of illumination when she receives an answer to
the problem of her meditation. The knowledge comes
unexpectedly in her colloquy, "What Can I Tell My
Bones?" (CP 172). What does she say to her bones when
she is sitting "In a world always late afternoon /
. . . / Longing for absolutes that never come"
(CP 171)? Her colloquy progresses in stages. At first
she is conscious of the soul as "A pulse beyond
nothingness, / A fearful ignorance," yet she "dares"
not take the ultimate leap: to "blaze like a tree"

(CP 171). Fearful that her "perpetual beginnings" may have thinned the substance of the soul (CP 171), she cries out: "The cause of God in me--has it gone?" (CP 172). Momentarily she wishes to escape, "to be delivered from the rational into the realm of pure song" (CP 172). The contemplative knows that the claims of reason will not bring him to God. The "realm of pure song" is that blessed condition in which one's being finally shares in the life of the eternal, when there is no longer any need for questions and answers. When the old woman thinks "God has need of me" (CP 172), things begin to alter and she affirms, "Existence dares perpetuate a soul" (CP 173).

Before the moment of reversal, however, the old woman is overwhelmed by anxiety. Her inner conflict is dramatized in Section 2 of the colloquy. Inner voices judge her:

The self says, I am;
The heart says, I am less;
The spirit says, you are nothing (CP 172).

The ego and the spirit vie for dominance while the heart beat reminds her that she is dying. The threat of nonbeing and the terror of meaningless are so great that she cries out in anguish:

The cause of God in me--has it gone?
Do these bones live? Can I live with these bones?
Mother, mother of us all, tell me where I am!
(CP 172).

One hears the echo of the dry bones of Ezekiel 37 that are revivified by the breath of God. Suddenly the old woman's tone alters. The arrangement of stanzas seems to indicate that these are the thoughts of the inner self:

```
To try to become like God
Is far from becoming God
O, but I seek and care!

I rock in my own dark,
Thinking, God has need of me.
The dead love the unborn (CP 172).
```

Roethke critics have speculated about what he means
when he speaks of becoming "like God."[8] A plausible
meaning is found in Roethke's notebooks, providing a
clue to Roethke's understanding of the nature of God:
"She's approaching the condition of God: she loves
everybody" (8 #110). God is the Eternal Principle of
Love that reaches out to man, desiring union with the
soul. As Underhill says, "The homeward journey of
man's spirit, then, may be thought of as due to the
push of a divine life within, answering to the divine
life without . . . 'God needs man,' says Eckhart. It
is Love calling love: (M 132-33). Roethke quotes
Eckhart in the notebooks: "God can no more do without
us than we can do without Him: (9 #121). In addition
to this reciprocal love and need, Roethke may have also
meant to imply the natural activity of mankind
searching for God. Meister Eckhart writes that" . . .
by nature, every creature seeks to become like God. If
there were no search for God, the heavens themselves
would not be revolving. . . . Covertly, nature seeks,
hunts, tries to ferret out the track on which God may
be found."[9] "I seek and care!" she says, as she
continues rocking in her own darkness.

The opening lines of section 3 signal the change
in the old woman's spiritual condition:

Weeds turn toward the wind weed-skeletons.
How slowly all things alter.

> Existence dares perpetuate a soul,
> A wedge of heaven's light, autumnal song
> (CP 173).

Her perpetual beginnings have not thinned the soul's substance. "Existence dares perpetuate a soul," she declares. Roethke's lady is "A prisoner of smells" who admits, "I would rather eat than pray," yet she finds that she is "released from the dreary dance of opposites" (CP 173). Her whole meditation has been reaching toward the moment when she would be able to proclaim: "I live in light's extreme; I stretch in all directions" (CP 173). The closing lines of the poem describe her rebirth:

> My spirit rises with the rising wind;
> I'm thick with leaves and tender as a dove,
> I take the liberties a short life permits—
> I seek my own meekness;
> I recover my tenderness by long looking.
> By midnight I love everything alive.
> Who took the darkness from the air?
> I'm wet with another life.
> Yea, I have gone and stayed (CP 173).

Surrendering herself to the light, the old woman exclaims: "The sun! The sun! And all we can become!" (CP 173). This submission creates a corresponding motion in which she embraces not only her surroundings but her own being as well. She begins by employing the agents of the soul to attain meekness. In his sermon, "Nothing above the Soul," Meister Eckhart outlines the "highest agents of the soul": "The first is intuition; the second, irascibilis, which is the upsurging agent; the third is the will."[10] Roethke's lady moves from an intution of "The bares speech of light among the stone" to a sense of living "in light's extreme" (CP 173).

Through the action of the upsurging agent her "spirit
rises with the rising wind." Finally the interior will
aids her in seeking meekness, interpreted by the author
of the fourteenth-century mystical treatise, The Cloud
of Unknowing, as "nought else but a true knowing and
feeling of man's self as he is" (11 #147). By "long
looking," the act of contemplation, the old woman
recovers her "tenderness" and with it a "love" for
"everything alive." Underhill defines contemplation
broadly as a "mental attitude under which all things
give up to us the secret of their life" (M 301; 12
#160). By long looking, then, the old woman
establishes communion with her inner self and the
natural world. Meekness, the condition of "humility"
which Roethke says is "the only possible attitude,"
prepares the old woman for the moment of release (11
#156). "Who took the darkness from the air?" she
asks. Suddenly she realizes that she is "wet with
another life," that her spirit has "gone and stayed."

>   What came to me vaguely is now clear,
>
>   As if released by a spirit,
>
>   Or agency outside me.
>
>   Unprayed-for,
>
>   And final (CP 173).

The old woman's stretch toward humility has
produced a state of "passive or infused contemplation"
which Underhill says is a "brief foretaste of the
Unitive State, often enjoyed for short periods in the
Illuminative Way" (M 245). "This act of contemplation," Underhill continues, "this glad surrender to
an overwhelming consciousness of the Presence of God,
leaves no sharp image on the mind: only a knowledge
that we have been lifted up to a veritable gazing upon
That which eye hath not seen" (M 244). Although

Roethke's lady does not speak of God, it is clear that she has been touched by the "Other," which she describes as "a spirit, / Or agency outside me." "I'm wet with another life," she says. "Unprayed-for," the release has been given, not willed. "Mystical intuition," as Charles Bennett has noted, "is the experience in which the solving idea 'dawns on' one, in which one discerns the clue, in which one recovers the forgotten subject of one's predicates."[11] The working of this intuition is implied in John Crowe Ransom's interpretation of the old woman's experience: "She has not had to pray for this revelation, and does not bother as to where it came from, being scarcely conscious of her metaphysics."[12] Those vague glimpses of "a reality more than the immediate" have been made clear and she has moved from darkness into light (SP 19). Now she knows what to tell her bones.

It is clear from Roethke's notebooks that during this period he was studying Underhill's Mysticism and Paul Tillich's The Courage to Be, 1952. He was thinking about existential anxiety and obviously reading Tillich as early as 1953. In a 1953 notebook he recorded these ideas:

Anxiety is awareness of the finite self as
    finite.

Anxiety about having to die: non-being is
    experienced from the inside (11 #147).

Though the old woman experiences anxiety about having to die, she is released "by a spirit, / Or agency outside [herself]" (CP 173). It is a release resulting from revelation, a moment of clarity, not an existential leap of faith as Rosemary Sullivan contends.[13] The old woman has experienced Illumination

of the Self, characterized by Underhill as an
"apprehension of the Infinite Life immanent in all
living things" (M 240). Underhill stresses that there
is an important distinction between the Illuminative
and the Unitive Life. In Illumination "The self,
though purified, still realizes itself as a separate
entity over against God. it is not immersed in its
Origin, but contemplates it" (M 240). In other words,
during Illumination, a person's "heightened
apprehension of reality lights up rather than
obliterates the rest of his life" (M 246). The nature
of the old woman's release resembles the "Intellectual
Vision" described by Underhill as "elusive, spiritual,
and formless," a vision which can occur during
Illumination (M 282). It is an ineffable vision which
"seems to be a something not sought but put before the
mind" [her italics], producing a feeling of the
presence of God in which the soul delights (M 282).
The old woman has experienced a rebirth and has become
conscious of the Eternal present in the universe.

       The nature of her revelation demonstrates
Roethke's belief in a symbolic relationship between the
natural and divine worlds. The key to his mystical
view of reality is revealed in this 1944-45 notebook
entry: "my symbol: revolving nexus: tie, link"
(5 #67). Nicolas Berdyaev (1874-1948), the Russian
religious philosopher, explains in Freedom and the
Spirit that this understanding of the universe is based
upon

         . . . the symbolism which admits the
      possibility of the transfusion of divine
      energy into this world, which binds together
      and unites two worlds, and recognizes that
      the Divine Being can only give symbolic

expression to Itself while it remains inexhaustible and mysterious.[14]

This conception of the worlds being bound together by the "transfusion of divine energy" is the origin of the mystical moments in Roethke's poetry.

As I indicated at the beginning of this chapter, the old woman's spiritual journey is analogous to the poetic experience in the soul of the poet. During creativity the poet engages in a concentration and expansion of the soul's powers, corresponding to the inward-and-outward movement of the self. As the inner self breaks into the field of consciousness, culminating in Illumination of the Self, so inspiration rises from the root of the soul to become the poetic intuition communicated in the poem. The spiritual activity at the end of the meditative sequence corresponds to the motion of poetic intuition or inspiration pervading the poet's being. The meaning or sense of the poem is equivalent, then, to poetic intuition, which is "subjectivity obscurely grasped in its very night together with some transapparent reality resounding in it."[15] Radiating from the depths of the soul, this meaning is the knowledge and experience grasped by the poet during the creative process--that is, the poet's subjectivity. It is this poetic knowledge that prepares for, or opens into, the poetic sense intuitively perceived in the "North American Sequence."

Once the poet's soul has grasped the subjective experience of the old woman--that existence dares perpetuate a soul and that it is possible to live in light's extreme--this poetic experience can be expanded further. Now that the inner self has been activated by an intuition of the Eternal omnipresent in the

temporal, the elemental opposites can be apprehended
through felt experience, ultimately creating unity of
being. Another journey within a journey occurs in the
"North American Sequence," but this time the speaker's
self is rooted in time and place, attaining the moving
stillness implied in "A Light Breather": "The spirit
moves, / Yet stays" (CP 101). Roethke's narrator
undergoes a "'journey towards the centre'" of which
Underhill speaks, but the path he takes does not
include a deliberate refusal of the messages of the
senses (M 302). As usual, Roethke's 'way of
introversion' is to permit the external eye to aid the
inner I, not to employ the will to gather the faculties
of the self in order to turn inward, "gazing into the
ground of the soul" (M 303). Roethke's speaker gazes
into the natural world, using the intuitive vision and
the soul's powers to gather the self in unity. The
speaker's specific desire is to transcend the sensual
emptiness represented by the spiritual decay of modern
American life, thereby finding a "way, the means of
establishing a personal identity, a self in the face of
that chaos" (SP 19). Whereas in "Meditations of an Old
Woman" Roethke was concerned with the third theme
mentioned in "On Identity'"--"The nature of creation,
that faculty for producing order out of disorder in the
arts, particularly in poetry" (SP 19)--he expands the
journey of the self in the "North American Sequence,"
illustrating the way the self can become "A body with
the motion of a soul" in the midst of the chaos of
modern life (CP 188).

IV

"NORTH AMERICAN SEQUENCE"

"O adorable actual: infinitizing life;
True mystic says life, not knowledge, is the
aim: Eternal life in the midst of time."
                    --Roethke Notebooks (6 #86)

"An obedience to the momentary reality,
which may, after all, be eternal!"
                    --Roethke Notebooks (10 #131)

Roethke's "North American Sequence" is an exploration of the "soul--the self of man setting its bearings in the total universe" (9 #129). The self referred to in this 1951 notebook entry is the inner self, the child or eternal spirit that spoke to the old woman in her sleep and played before her as in a dream. During this stage of the struggle for selfhood, however, the narrator not only apprehends the eternal child in a state of reverie but also sees it stand outside himself--"As if another man appeared out of the depths of my being"--transforming the speaker into "A something wholly other" (CP 205). The reappearance of the child and the emergence of the man are part of the "cyclic" method Roethke mentions in "Open Letter," the recurrence of profound experiences, "with variation and change, each time bringing us closer to our own most particular (and thus most universal) reality" (SP 39). In this part of the cycle the narrator contemplates "his own immensity," both his death and his infinitude, and becomes "the final man," one who is complete and whole (CP 201). Spiritual equilibrium is achieved as the true self is established in the moving stillness of the "rose in the sea-wind"--setting its bearings in the total universe (CP 205).

This journey through the American landscape is at
once a psychological and spiritual journey. The
sequence may be described as a meditative song cycle,
six lyrics depicting "the long journey out of the self"
which is simultaneously a "Journey to the Interior," to
the deeper self (CP 193). The necessity for such a
trip, by automobile or memory, is disclosed in one of
Roethke's 1942 notebooks: "How far one can journey
from the true self, the heart's centre: the resolve"
(3 #28). The resolve, of course, is to discover or
reclaim the "hidden self" that "lives a 'substantial'
life in touch with the real or transcendental world"
(M 67). By recovering the self the speaker of the
sequence hopes to create "a body with the motion of the
soul" (CP 188). Once he becomes aware of the deeper
self, once it emerges into the conscious life, he will
attain unity of being or selfhood. Roethke even
indicates in "On Identity'" that this striving to know
the self may create a corresponding motion in which the
self becomes a pure soul: "Should we say the self,
once perceived, becomes the soul?" (SP 21).
Endeavoring to become a spiritual being, the speaker of
the "North American Sequence" immerses himself in the
flow of life, learning that "All finite things reveal
infinitude" (CP 201). The six lyrics which move the
mind toward this moment develop according to the
meditative process: composition, analysis and
colloquy. The opening preludes are found in the first
poem, "The Longing." "Meditation at Oyster River"
seems to be a transition lyric in that it continues the
preludes and begins the speaker's self-analysis. The
remaining four poems comprise the major discourses
which are essentially colloquies with the self. The
speaker is assisted in his journey by several agents:

memory, imagination, will, the external eye penetrating the natural world, and the hidden self breaking gradually into his consciousness. These faculties precipitate the insights which guide the narrator in creating an interior order, a new sense of self.

Like the old woman's meditation, the "North American Sequence" begins with the prelude, "composition of place." Once again Roethke employs concrete physical details to portray spiritual emptiness and decay. The speaker of "The Longing" exists in "A kingdom of stinks and sighs" where there is "no balm," only "Agony of crucifixion on barstools" (CP 187). In this city where "Lust fatigues the soul," he wonders "How to transcend this sensual emptiness?" (CP 187).

This question establishes the general direction of the meditation, a subject that will be clarified in the following poem. So little life-giving energy is present in this world that "The great trees no longer shimmer; / Not even the soot dances" (CP 187). Small wonder that the spirit is inert:

> And the spirit fails to move forward,
> But shrinks into a half-life, less than
>   itself,
> Falls back, a slug, a loose worm
> Ready for any crevice,
> An eyeless starer. (CP 187)

The "inner I" or deeper self is caught far below the threshold of his consciousness and "fails to move forward." The spirit is "An eyeless starer," for the self has not become the soul, reflected in the eye of God. "A wretch needs his wretchedness," the narrator acknowledges in Section 2, for "Out of these nothings / --All beginnings come" (CP 188). If he can overcome

the "pride" of the phenomenal self, the spirit will
move forward to create the "felicity" of "A body with
the motion of a soul" (CP 188). His hope of renewal is
symbolized by the rose that "exceeds us all"
(CP 188). In order to "transcend this sensual
emptiness" he would simplify the self by penetrating
the natural world. His longing, then, is to "be beyond
the moon, / Bare as a bud, and naked as a worm"
(CP 188).

In Section 3, the second prelude, Roethke
catalogues in the manner of Whitman that the speaker
"would" do and be in order to move the spirit forward:

> I would with the fish, the blackening
>   salmon, and the mad lemmings,
> The children dancing, the flowers
> widening.
>
> . . . .
>
> I would unlearn the lingo of
>   exasperation, all the distortions of
>   malice and hatred;
> I would believe my pain: and the eye
>   quiet on the growing rose;
> I would delight in my hands, the branch
>   singing, altering the excessive bird;
> I long for the imperishable quiet at the
>   heart of form;
> I would be a stream, winding between
>   great striated rocks in late
>   summer. . .
>   CP 188).

To aid the spirit's progress he would abandon the
distorting language of exasperation, learning instead
the way of the fish and dancing children. He would
embrace the free movement of the natural processes of

life, including accepting his pain. Assisting the
"inner I," the external eye would meditate on the
growing rose, symbolic of "the imperishable quiet at
the heart of form," watching the motion of the spirit
that "moves, / Yet stays" (CP 101). At the same time,
he would delight "in the redolent disorder of this
mortal life," immersing himself in "This ambush, this
silence," knowing that there "shadow can change into
flame" (CP 188). "What dream's enough to breath in?"
he had asked earlier: "A dark dream" (CP 188). This
breath of a flame, the possibility of light, awaits in
this stagnant city amid the "Fetor of cockroaches, dead
fish, petroleum" (CP 187).

Having seen "A great flame" rising from "the
sunless sea," the narrator leaves "the body of the
whale," but "the mouth of the night" is still open wide
before him--the darkness of America's past depicted by
the "smell" of buffalo fur "drying in the sun" (CP 188-
89). Wondering if "Old men should be explorers," he
decides to be a primitive Iroquois Indian, one who
lives close to water. There he would find a way to
renew the spirit. Roethke comments on the narrator's
symbolic journey in the notebooks:[1]

> Now a longer piece in which the
> protagonist faces the horrors of the
> modern city, rises out of his own spirit
> to achieve an equanimity with an earlier
> more primitive American life--the world
> of the fish, the bird, the child, the
> Indian (13 #192).

Roethke hopes that his speaker will journey from the
bleakness "at the edge of the raw cities" to recover
the sense of rootedness at the core of his being,
thereby creating a condition of serenity comparable to

that known by the child (CP 187). His way, as we shall
see, is to contemplate natural processes, to know the
fish and the bird as an Iroquois would and to attain
the harmony of the growing rose.

"Meditation at Oyster River" is a prelude to "the
long journey out of the self," another description of
the narrator's longing to attain unity of being. Its
meditative technique demonstrates the importance of
recollection to the stirring of the spirit. This
quotation recorded in a notebook of the early 1940's
reflects the significance Roethke placed upon
meditation:

> 'Everything will be found to hinge
> finally on the idea of meditation. This
> idea has suffered a steady decline in
> the Occident, along with the
> transcendent view of life in general
> . . . yet it is not certain that
> religion itself can survive unless men
> retain some sense of the wisdom which
> may be won by sitting in quiet
> recollection' (5 #63).

"Recollection," as Roethke says in a 1951-52 entry,
requires "disciplining and simplifying of the
attention," a gathering of the faculties in
concentration (9 #120). Such meditation produces a way
of seeing in which correspondences are apprehended; the
poet explains in a 1958 notebook:

> So I would be: not only to perceive the
> single thing sharply: but to perceive
> the relationships between many things
> sharply perceived (13 #176).

The speaker's recollections at Oyster River move the
spirit for a time, leading him to consider the grace
the self can assume and the way the will may journey.

The poem opens upon a twilight scene, the speaker
sitting "in the deepening light" watching "the first
tide-ripples" of the blue-black river "moving, almost
without sound" (CP 190). In this place where there is
"No sound from the bay, No violence," where even the
gulls are silent and the wind is slackening (CP 190),
the speaker begins to confront "the redolent disorder
of this mortal life, / This ambush, this silence"
(CP 188). He acknowledges that "The self persists like
a dying star, / In sleep, afraid" (CP 190). The
phenomenal self, the ego, afraid to face the ambush of
life with the insouciance of the deer or the
hummingbird, persists in holding on to its identity
"like a dying star." Knowing that he should be like
the rose the "exceeds us all," the speaker yearns to be
one "with water" and "the shy beasts." "Death's face
rises afresh, / Among the shy beasts" each day, yet the
doe continues "loping across the highway," and the
hummingbird does not stop "whirring from quince-blossom
to morning-glory" (CP 190). So, too, the waves move
forward "without cessation" despite the fact that they
are "altered by sand-bars, beds of kelp, miscellaneous
driftwood" (CP 191). Reflecting upon these images of
the self's involvement in the cycle of life, the
speaker momentarily "takes on the pure poise of the
spirit":

In this hour,
In this first heaven of knowing,

> The flesh takes on the pure poise of the
>   spirit,
> Acquires, for a time, the sandpiper's
>   insouciance,
> The hummingbird's surety, the kingfisher's
>   cunning. (CP 191)

This new-found assurance provokes the memory of other
beginnings, scenes of movement and change. Quite
naturally the recollections are of water: "Of the
first trembling of a Michigan brook in April, / Over a
lip of stone" and of "the Tittebawasee, in the time
between winter and spring, / When the ice melts along
the edges of early afternoon" (CP 191). These
beginnings prepare for an image which is Roethke's most
explicit representation of the speaker's desire to move
beyond spiritual stasis:

> And I long for the blast of dynamite,
> The sudden sucking roar as the culvert
>   loosens its debris of branches and sticks,
> Welter of tin cans, pails, old bird nests, a
>   child's shoe riding a log,
> As the piled ice breaks away from the
>   battered spiles,
> And the whole river begins to move forward,
>   its bridges shaking (CP 191).

Just as the blast of dynamite causes the ice to break
away and the river to move forward, so the speaker's
baptism by water will cause the deep self to break
through the threshold of consciousness and the unified
self to press beyond itself. By immersing himself in
the water, by becoming one with the winding stream, he
hopes to participate in the harmony and strife which
will contribute to the growth of the self.

This meditation on the possibility of the self breaking away from its fear, that it may not persist "like a dying star," causes the speaker to "rock with the motion of morning" (CP 191). Sitting still on a rock "in the cradle of all that is," he is "lulled" into a state of reverie by the motion of the water and the "Cries of the sandpiper" (CP 191). In this final section of the poem, the speaker takes on the moving stillness of a man who is in complete harmony with the sea. Out of this half-sleep and this motion come the spirit and the speaker's resolve. "Water's my will, and my way," he declares as he watches "the spirit" running "In and out of the small waves" (CP 192). Once again "the small" are his teachers, for the spirit plays with "the intrepid shorebirds" who are "graceful" in the face of "danger" (CP 192). One is reminded of Roethke's comment in a 1955 notebook that "Our movement toward the small [is] a holy thing: a stretch toward humility" (12 #163). The grace of the "intrepid shorebirds" will become the way of the self in the face of death. Scattering its first light, the moon shines at the end of the poem, preparing for "the long journey out of the self."

Having awakened the soul's agents in the opening preludes, the speaker is now guided through his analytical discourses by memory (imagination) and the external eye, both fostering an intuitive vision which animates the deeper self. In "Journey to the Interior" the speaker's journey out of the phenomenal self to the inner self is depicted through the descriptions of two automobile trips. Both journeys are symbolic of psychic landscapes. The first is a dead-end trip with "many detours, washed-out interrupted raw places / Where the shale slides" and the car almost backs over

the edge. He drives cautiously. "Better to hug close,
wary of rubble and falling stone," he says (CP 193).
The path narrows, "winding upward toward the stream
with its sharp stone." It passes "Through the swamp
alive with quicksand," ending in dark thickets and ugly
ravines (CP 193). The second journey is a remembered
"drive in gravel, / Watching for dangerous down-hill
places, where the wheels whined beyond eighty" (CP
193). This time he drives more recklessly because "the
road was part of me, and its ditches" (CP 193). Scenes
of Midwestern America flow past in the mind: "The
cemetery with two scrubby trees in the middle of the
prairie / . . . / The floating hawks, the jackrabbits,
the grazing cattle" (CP 194). The sun appears "over
the Tetons" and he rises and falls "in the slow sea of
a grassy plain" (CP 194). His reverie produces a
meditative state in which he experiences the Eternal
Now:

> I rise and fall, and time folds
>
> Into a long moment;
>
> And I hear the lichen speak,
>
> And the ivy advance with its white lizard
>
>   feet--
>
> On the shimmering road,
>
> On the dusty detour (CP 194).

The upward and downward journeys imagined in the mind
have produced a sense of rising and falling, opposites
which are reconciled in the folding or stretching of
the eternal now-moment. When "time folds / Into a long
moment" the eternal intersects the temporal and the way
up becomes the way down, rising and falling are one.

Roethke's perception of time may appear to be
informed by this passage from Meister Eckhart quoted in
a 1951-52 notebook:

> Neither time nor space, neither before
> nor after, but everything present is one
> new,   fresh-springing   Now,   where
> milleniums   last   no   longer   than   the
> twinkling of an eye (9 #129).

But for Eckhart, the "present Now-moment" is a moment
above or beyond time in which God's Son is brought to
birth in the soul.   It is a moment when the soul is
rapt out of time into the Eternal Now:

> There is a difference between the soul's
> day and God's day but in the day most
> native to the soul, it perceives things
> from above all space and time, and finds
> them neither near nor far away. . . .
> God created the world and everything in
> it in the one present Now. . . .   The
> soul that lives in the present Now-
> moment is the soul in which the Father
> begets his only begotten Son and in that
> birth the soul is born again.   It is
> still one birth, however often the soul
> is reborn in God, as the Father begets
> his only begotten Son.[2]

Roethke, on the other hand, perceives the present as a
"fresh-springing Now" because, as Tillich puts it, "The
eternal stops the flux of time" and "provides for us a
temporal 'now.'"   Although there is no evidence that
Roethke read Tillich's The Eternal Now, a passage from
Tillich helps to clarify Roethke's understanding of the
relationship between time and eternity:

> But the world, by its very nature, is
> that which comes to and end. . . .
> There is no time after time, but there
> is   eternity   above   time

[his italics] . . . every moment of time
reaches into the eternal. It is the
eternal that stops the flux of time for
us. It is the eternal "now" which
provides for us a temporal "now." . .
. Not everybody, and nobody all the
time, is aware of this "eternal now" in
the temporal "now." But sometimes it
breaks powerfully into our consciousness
and gives us the certainty of the
eternal, of a dimension of time which
cuts into time and gives us our time.[3]

For Roethke, time "folds" or reaches into the eternal,
creating the eternal now-moment.

In this moment of heightened meditation, the
narrator's perception of creative energy is sharply
increased and he hears "the lichen speak" and "the ivy
advance." This experience causes a vision of "the
flower of all water" to break into his consciousness:

I see the flower of all water, above and
    below me, the never receding,
Moving, unmoving in a parched land, white in
    the moonlight:
The soul at a still-stand,
At ease after rocking the flesh to sleep,
Petals and reflections of petals mixed on the
    surface of a glassy pool,
And the waves flattening out when the
    fishermen drag their nets over the stones
                    (CP 194).

The "flower of all water . . . / Moving, unmoving in a
parched land" foreshadows and opens into the revelation
of the "rose in the sea-wind" at the end of the

sequence, "rooted in stone, keeping the whole of light" (CP 205). Both images depict that moving stillness which is "the imperishable quiet at the heart of form"--"A body with the motion of a soul" (CP 188). In a 1957-58 notebook Roethke comments that "The soul is the form, or essential and constituent principle of man" (12 #172). When the deeper self is perceived the body is informed by the soul and comes upon "the true ease of [itself]" (CP 205). This is the condition of rootedness suggested in "The soul at a still-stand," not a state of calmness implying stagnation but rather the stillness-in-motion of the rose in the sea-wind. The colon in the lines above connects the flower and the soul, making the "soul at a still-stand" a vision of the inner self, "the flower of all water . . . / Moving, unmoving in a parched land."

The following stanza prepares for the speaker's stretch toward death, that moment when he seems to become the "soul: horizon between time and eternity" (9 #129) and stands, confronting his death.

> In the moment of time when the small drop
>   forms, but does not fall,
> I have known the heart of the sun,--
> In the dark and light of a dry place,
> In a flicker of fire brisked by a dusty wind.
> I have heard, in a drip of leaves,
> A slight song,
> After the midnight cries (CP 194).

Moments when he has "known the heart of the sun"--the creative source of life--have been moments "of time" when motion has gathered to a stillness or fire has been "brisked by a dusty wind." At such times, when opposites have suddenly come into place, he has heard "A slight song" in the water dripping from the

leaves. This remembered perception of the presence of
the eternal in the midst of time and change leads the
speaker to meditate upon the ultimate change, death.
He "rehearses" by standing "at the stretch in the face
of death, / Delighting in surface change, the glitter
of light on waves" (CP 195). Turning toward the other
side of light," he meditates "Unperplexed, in a place
leading nowhere" (CP 195). The act of stretching
toward eternity exerts the will "And I roam elsewhere,
my body thinking" (CP 195). To think with the body, as
Roethke says in "On Identity,'" is to feel, to foster
the intuitive vision.

Thus by meditating intuitively, the speaker
uncomplicates the mind and is brought to a place
"Neither forward nor backward," a place which is at
once nowhere and everywhere. From this eternal place
the speaker comes to a realization:

> As a blind man, lifting a curtain, knows it
>   is morning,
> I know this change:
> On one side of silence there is no smile;
> But when I breathe with the birds,
> The spirit of wrath becomes the spirit of
>   blessing,
> And the dead begin from their dark to sing in
>   my sleep (CP 195).

Traditionally birds have suggested the spiritual, as
opposed to the material; they have even symbolized the
winged soul. Thus when he takes on the spiritual, when
he breathes with the breath of a pure soul, wrath is
transformed into blessing: the changes that occur with
the passage of time are felt to be holy and life-
giving, not threatening or destructive, and even the
dead come to his aid, singing.

In "The Long Waters" the speaker experiences spiritual Awakening, losing and finding himself in "a rich desolation of wind and water . . . a landlocked bay, where the salt water is freshened" (CP 197). Aided by memory and the eyes meditating on this place, he moves from the temporal world of change to an intuition of the "Numinous: impalpable spirituality" (10 #135)--"The numinous ring around the opening flower" (CP 198).[4] His analytical discourse, a colloquy with the self "Where the fresh and salt waters meet," creates the moment at the end of the poem when the inner self or spirit runs before him and he achieves a sense of wholeness.

At the beginning of the poem he turns affirmatively to the small: to the minnows who can hear and the butterflies who "Rejoice in the language of smells and dancing" (CP 196). He proceeds to "reject" the sensual "world of the dog" and to "acknowledge [his] foolishness with God":

My desire for the peaks, the black ravines,
   the rolling mists
Changing with every twist of wind,
The unsinging fields where no lungs breathe,
Where light is stone (CP 196).

The tone of self-mockery assumed by the narrator is actually Roethke's voice confessing his life-long infatuation with God, an unreasoning attraction that turned from a need into a hunt, and acknowledging his longing for the peaks and the ravines--the full range of mystical experience. As he comments in a 1949 notebook, "Dear God, I want it all: the depths and heights" (8 #110). Nicolas Berdyaev writes that "Only the depths and heights of the spiritual life deserve the name of mysticism, for it is there that man

penetrates to the ultimate mystery."[5]   Instead of
mounting to God by transcending this world, Roethke's
speaker, and I would maintain Roethke as well, has
chosen to discover the Eternal by establishing an
"I-Thou" relationship with the natural world:[6]

> I return where fire has been
> To the charred edge of the sea
> Where the yellowish prongs of grass poke
>   through the blackened ash,
> And the bunched logs peel in the afternoon
>   sunlight,
> Where the fresh and salt waters meet,
> And the sea-winds move through the pine
>   trees,
> A country of bays and inlets, and small
>   streams flowing seaward (CP 196).

He returns where fire and water, fresh and salt water
meet, for it is there that he receives glimpses of the
Eternal Thou.   It is there where the temporal and the
eternal meet that he learns of the changing self.

At times the self still fearfully views nature as
purely destructive.   The narrator calls upon "Mnetha,
Mother of Har," the wise nurse in Blake's Tiriel, to
"protect" him "From the worm's advance and retreat,
from the butterfly's havoc / . . . / The dubious sea-
change, the heaving sands, and my tentacled sea-
cousins" (CP 196).   He invokes Mnetha, whose name
implies wisdom founded upon memory,[7] to be with him
when he sees natural processes as flux without order,
change without purpose.   "Blessed by the lips of a low
wind," symbolic of the Spirit, he comes to the place
where salt and fresh water meet, a "rich desolation of
wind and water" (CP 197).   He watches the waves and
remembers:

> I remember a stone breaking the eddying
>   current,
> Neither white nor red, in the dead middle
>   way,
> Where impulse no longer dictates, nor the
>   darkening shadow,
> A vulnerable place,
> Surrounded by sand, broken shells, the
>   wreckage of water (CP 197).

This memory of the "stone breaking the eddying current" in "A vulnerable place" prepares for the revelation at the end of the poem.

The self feels vulnerable before "the wreckage of water," but in Section 5 " the sea wind wakes desire"; moved by the spirit, he becomes "another thing":

> I see in the advancing and retreating waters
> The shape that came from my sleep, weeping:
> The eternal one, the child, the swaying vine
>   branch,
> The numinous ring around the opening flower,
> The friend that runs before me on the windy
>   headlands,
> Neither voice nor vision (CP 198).

The weeping shape that emerges is the eternal child, "The friend that runs before me . . . / Neither voice nor vision." Roethke uses this archetypal figure to symbolize the deep self breaking through the threshhold of consciousness. When this buried life rises from the unconscious, the narrator becomes a new being:

> I, who came back from the depths laughing too
>   loudly,
> Became another thing;
> My eyes extend beyond the farthest bloom of
>   the waves;

I lose and find myself in the long water;

I am gathered together once more;

I embrace the world (CP 198).

He loses the phenomenal self and finds the true self
"in the long water." This act recreates the self,
causing him to extend beyond the self to embrace the
entire world.

The Awakening of the Self at the end of "The long
Waters" marks the turning point in the colloquies and
the meditative sequence as a whole. The speaker's
intuition of "The numinous ring around the open flower"
prepares for the realization in the next colloquy that
"All finite things reveal infinitude" (CP 201).
Moreover, the emergence of the eternal child prefigures
the transformation of the "lost self" into "the final
man," one who reconciles life and death, time and
eternity (CP 201). During the colloquies, the
speaker's meditations on the elements of existence,
particularly the manner in which they converge to
reveal their opposition, lead to higher levels of
understanding whereby the opposites are reconciled,
folding into the "rose in the sea-wind" at the end of
the sequence (CP 105). These discourses with the self
have progressed gradually from the folding of time into
an eternal Now and the apprehension of "the flower of
all water" to the release of the spirit and the
stirring of the will to embrace the world. Continuing
to contemplate the processes of earth and air, the
speaker ultimately moves beyond his fear of death to
"rejoice in being what I was," a unified self
(CP 205). Having gathered himself together in "The
Long Waters," the speaker will be able to become
"Something wholly other" at the end of the sequence,
"Rooted in stone, keeping the while of light" (CP 205).

The journey motif is repeated at the beginning of
"The Far Field" as the speaker dreams of deadends: "Of
flying like a bat deep into a narrowing tunnel" or "Of
driving alone," ending with the car stalled in a
snowdrift (CP 199). Whereas earlier he had focused on
upward and downward journeys corresponding to his "rise
and fall in the slow sea of a grassy plain" (CP 194),
now the flight into the narrowing tunnel initiates a
meditation on the death of nature, endings which
ultimately speak of beginnings. Just as the way down
is the way up, so the way out of this "sensual
emptiness" is the way into the tunnel, an exploration
of the passage from death to life.

By observing the movement of life that culminates
in decay and death, the speaker is renewed by thought
of his own death. He journeys to the past, returning
to the field behind his father's house. There where
life and death are juxtaposed he learns of the eternal:

> At the field's end, in the corner missed by
>   the mower,
> Where the turf drops off into a grass-hidden
>   culvert,
> Haunt of the cat-bird, nesting-place of the
>   field-mouse,
> Not too far away from the ever-changing
>   flower-dump,
> Among the tin cans, tires, rusted pipes,
>   broken machinery,--
> One learned of the eternal;
> And in the shrunken face of a dead rat, eaten
>   by rain and ground-beetles (CP 199).

All living things die eventually. Even the tin cans
rust and machinery breaks down. The flower-dump is
"ever-changing," for flowers continue to blossom and

wither.   "I suffered for birds," he says, and "for
young rabbits caught in the mower" (CP 199).   But his
"grief" is not "excessive," for when he hears "warblers
in early May" or watches their "fearless" flight in and
out of the tree, he "forget[s] time and death"
(CP 200).   Although the speaker has not met the
Changeless One, he has seen the enduring cycle of life
and death.   He begins "thinking" of the beginning of
creation and ends "Believing" in his own reincarnation:
"I'll return again, / As a snake or a raucous bird"
(CP 200).   The revelation in the field teaches him not
to fear his own death:

> I learned not to fear infinity,
> The far field, the windy cliffs of forever,
> The dying of time in the white light of
>   tomorrow,
> The wheel turning away from itself,
> The sprawl of the wave,
> The on-coming water (CP 200).

The outward turning motion of the wheel and the "on-
coming" wave produce a corresponding motion in the
speaker whereby he comes upon the still center of his
being.   Just as "The river turns on itself," and "The
tree retreats into its own shadow," so the speaker
feels "a weightless change" which is an ingoing as well
as "a moving forward" (CP 200).

     This change signifies the speaker's movement into
a higher state of consciousness, the stage of Interior
Silence.   The meditative process has brought him to "a
still, but not a deep center," he says: "A point
outside the glittering current," the flow of life (CP
201).   This quiet point is the center of the self, the
soul--the point on the horizon where time and eternity

meet, the vantage point from which he is "renewed by death":

> I am renewed by death, thought of my death,
> The dry scent of a dying garden in September,
> The wind fanning the ash of a low fire.
> What I love is near at hand,
> Always, in earth and air (CP 201).

In accepting his death, the speaker not only experiences a renewal but also recognizes the eternal working in the never-ending processes of earth, wind and fire. Therefore he loves what is "near at hand," that which is "Always, in earth and air." It is in the field near at hand, not "The far field," that he learns of the "adorable actual: infinitizing life" (6 #86).

The change that occurs in the "lost self" at the end of the poem is symbolic of the speaker's Purification of the Self, the fruit of Interior Silence. Out of the imagination comes the revelation of "A sea-shape"--"An old man with his feet before the fire, / In robes of green, in garments of adieu" (CP 201). Though his "robes of green" clearly celebrate beginnings as well as endings, the speaker says "He is the end of things, the final man" (CP 201). The key to this figure is the fact that he contains within himself "The pure serene of memory"--"A ripple widening from a single stone / Winding around the waters of the world" (CP 201). The speaker has undergone a process of self-simplification by reducing the self to its essentials, stretching it like a violin string until it is a pure melody. In this way he has taken on the poise of the spirit, becoming a serene being that remembers all, folding into itself life and death. Thus he not only possesses racial memory, he begins and ends the circle of infinity as well.

Roethke's "final man" is a primordial figure
representing the "lost self" transformed into the wise
man who, having confronted his death, possesses the
final knowledge: "All finite things reveal infinitude"
(CP 201).[8] Now that the speaker has been "faced with
his own immensity," his own stretch into infinity, he
has become the "final man" for whom "The murmur of the
absolute, the why / Of being born fails on his naked
ears" (CP 201). He has attained a simplicity of being
which exceeds the necessity of questions, the
requirement of answers.

The essence of the speaker's wisdom is stressed in
an early version of the poem found in Roethke's
notebooks:

The temporal interplay
Renewal,
Perpetual renewal,
All finite things reveal infinitude
                    (13 #185).

This intuition of an enduring quality in all things by
which they are made new prepares for the Illumination
of the Self at the end of the colloquy. In her
discussion of Illumination, Underhill quotes this
passage from the writings of William Law:

Everything in temporal nature is
descended out of that which is eternal,
and stands as a palpable invisible
outbirth of it, so when we know how to
separate the grossness, death, and
darkness of time from it, we find what
it is in its eternal state . . . (M
263).

Such clarity of vision comes, Blake tells us, when "the doors of perception are cleansed" so that "everything appears to man as it is, infinite."[9]

In the final colloquy, "The Rose," the speaker's use of Ordinary Contemplation produces Illumination of the Self. He contemplates in a place which is reminiscent of the setting of "The Long Waters," an "important" place, he says, "Where sea and fresh water meet" (CP 202). During "Meditation at Oyster River" he had contemplated sitting on a rock, the gulls "Silent, in the deepening light" (CP 190). Watching the motion of the water, he attained "this first heaven of knowing" when "The flesh takes on the pure poise of the spirit" (CP 191). Out of his reverie at the river's edge came the recognition that "Water's my will, and my way" (CP 192). Later, the spirit guided him to "the charred edge of the sea," a place "Where the fresh and salt waters meet" (CP 196). In that place, "a rich desolation of wind and water," the eternal child appeared (CP 197). Not until now, however, has the speaker specifically said that "this place," a place where the eternal is revealed, is "important." It is here in a state of Quiet that the "inner I" emerges and establishes itself, even as the rose gathers into itself the elements representing the material and spiritual worlds. Coming upon "the true ease of [himself]" he achieves unity of being (CP 205).

In this place where "hawks sway out into the wind," the inner self appears: "I sway outside myself / Into the darkening current," the speaker says (CP 202). Is this the place, he wonders, where he was once a pure spirit, wearing a "crown of birds for a moment," where "The light heightened" and "The first rain gathered" (CP 202)? The rose is found in this

place of spiritual beginnings. In Section 2 Roethke
contrasts the motion of a ship sailing in a light wind,
symbolic of the continuous human journey, with the
moving stillness of "the rose in the sea-wind" that
"Stays in its true place" yet extends beyond itself:

> Flowering out of the dark,
> Widening at high noon, face upward,
> A single wild rose, struggling out of the
>   white embrace of the morning-glory,
> Out of the briary hedge, the tangle of matted
>   underbrush,
> Beyond the clover, the ragged hay,
> Beyond the sea pine, the oak, the wind-tipped
>   madrona,
> Moving with the waves . . . (CP 203).

This rose that "exceeds us all" provokes a greenhouse
memory from his childhood:

> And I think of roses, roses,
> White and red, in the wide six-hundred-foot
>   greenhouses,
> And my father standing astride the cement
>   benches,
> Lifting me high over the four-foot stems, the
>   Mrs. Russells, and his own elaborate
>   hybrids,
> And how those flowerheads seemed to flow
>   toward me, to beckon me, only a child, out
>   of myself (CP 203).

The child to whom the father and the roses seem to be
beckoning becomes the eternal child, "The friend that
runs before me on the windy headlands, / Neither voice
nor vision" (CP 198). It is the same "true self" that
runs "toward a Hill" in "Once more, the Round" at the
end of the "Sequence, Sometimes Metaphysical"

(CP 251). "What need for heaven, then, / With that
man, and those roses?" Roethke's speaker says, for the
meeting of father and son has created an eternal now-
moment.[10]

In Section 3 Roethke juxtaposes "sound and
silence": the sounds of America--birds, bulldozers,
car horns--and "the single sound" when "light enters
the sleeping soul" (CP 204). The sounds swell from the
lyrical song of a single thrush to the piercing cry of
the cicada, from the whistle of the Killdeer to "The
shriek of nails as old shingles are ripped from the top
of a roof" (CP 204). Suddenly the sounds diminish to
"the twittering of swallows above water" and the thin
sound of the mind remembering "all," causing the light
to enter "gently" into "the sleeping soul." "Beautiful
my desire, and the place of my desire," the speaker
says (CP 204). It is through place that the mind
remembers the All and light illumines the soul, moving
the will. The speaker's thoughts turn to moments of
quiet expectancy, those times when nature is gathered
to a great stillness, resonant with new
possibilities. He thinks of "the rock singing, and
light making its own silence, / At the edge of a
ripening meadow, in early summer" (CP 204). All of
nature is on "the edge," caught in a state of becoming,
waiting for change. It is "that lonely time" between
night and "the breaking of morning" when "the moon
lingers" and raindrops hang on leaves, "Shifting in the
wakening sunlight / Like the eyes of a new-caught fish"
(CP 204]. These images of nature caught between
becoming and being anticipate the state of being
achieved by the speaker at the end of the poem. He
becomes that pleased rock lighted from within,
embracing sound and silence. This condition of Quiet

produces the illuminated vision at the end of the
sequence.

In the final section, the speaker returns to the
sea, reminding us that he lives "with the rocks / . . .
/ their holes / Cut by the sea-slime" (CP 205). In a
"grove of sun-parched, wind-warped madrona, / Among the
half-dead trees," near a rose growing out of the
sea-slime, he comes "upon the true ease of [himself]"
(CP 205). It was "As if another man appeared out of
the depths of my being," the speaker says (CP 205).
The deep self emerges and stands outside the phenomenal
self, "Beyond becoming and perishing," and the speaker
becomes "A something wholly other," a moving stillness
(CP 205). Like the motion of the spirit in "A Light
Breather," he has gone and stayed. His spirit has
"swayed out on the wildest wave alive" and yet he has
remained still (CP 205).

The meditative sequence culminates in the
revelation of the "rose in the sea-wind," an image of
ordered perfection which draws together and balances
the tensions within the narrator and the sequence.
This rose is a concrete symbol, not the abstract rose
of Dante, Yeats and Eliot, yet it resounds with
metaphysical overtones. Roethke defines "Rose" in a
1962-63 notebook as "spiritual love and supreme
beauty," and even lists pairs of opposites--"matter and
spirit, time and eternity, death and rebirth, man and
God"--perhaps implying their reconciliation in the rose
(15 #218). In the sequence, however, "this rose in the
sea-wind" is associated with a memory of the roses in
the greenhouse of Roethke's father, suggesting that the
symbol is also personal. Thus, the rose seems to
embrace the material and the spiritual, representing a
balance between the natural and divine worlds.[11] Since

its first appearance in "The Longing" as the rose that
"exceeds us all," this "flower of all water" has
gathered significance, and has become a rich,
affirmative symbol of the nature of being--free, stable
and harmonious. It embodies the spiritual equilibrium
which the narrator has achieved, a condition of
stillness-in-motion. Perceiving this rose, he is
released from spiritual emptiness and despair and
rejoices in his new sense of self:

> And I rejoiced in being what I was:
> In the lilac change, the white reptilian
> calm,
> In the bird beyond the bough, the single one
> With all the air to greet him as he flies,
> The dolphin rising from the darkening waves;
>
> And in this rose, this rose in the sea-wind,
> Rooted in stone, keeping the whole of light,
> Gathering to itself sound and silence--
> Mine and the sea-wind's (CP 205).

Underhill states that Pure Being manifests itself
in two characteristic ways:

> It shows itself to us as Power by means
> of strife, of the struggle and
> opposition of its own qualities. But it
> shows itself to us as Reality, in
> harmonizing and reconciling within
> itself these discordant opposites
> (M 40).

As Roethke records in a 1950 notebook, no doubt quoting
Heraclitus, a pre-Socratic philosopher, "'The highest
harmony springs from opposites and all things are in a
state of strife'" (9 #118).[12] Whereas the old woman
was "released from the dreary dance of opposites"

(CP 173), the speaker in the "North American Sequence" experiences them until they suddenly come into place. The speaker's inner unity and the poem's harmony are embodied in the rose that gathers to itself and reconciles the opposites of the sequence: earth and water (land and sea), fire and shadow, stone and wind, salt and fresh water.[13]   These elements represent the opposition between motion and stillness, fluidity and order, time and eternity.   The speaker has been stretching between these concepts, meditating upon the nature of being and nonbeing.   Just as the rose folds the opposites into itself, "keeping the whole of light," so there is a higher and lower merging of the speaker's self, producing unity of being.   Thus, the "rose in the sea-wind, / Rooted in stone" is the realization of the "imperishable quiet at the heart of form," the centrality of being sought by the speaker.

The meaning of the speaker's journey is presented by Roethke in the following stanza, an early revision of the poem recorded in a 1961-62 notebook:

I have partaken of the heavenly food;
I have received the message from the place of
    perfection--
But what do I do now, facing the foam
    on the shore, under the parched madrona
    with its crown of birds--
Let the moon walk over me?   I have found my
    deeper life (14, #206).

The speaker has reached the deep center of the self by apprehending the eternal in the temporal.   This intuition of the numinous, the holy, in the midst of time is echoed in a quotation recorded in a 1951 notebook:

'Eternity is the experience of holding
and possessing in one moment the here
and now, the past and present and that
which is to come.' There are times,
yes, when reality comes closer (9 #121).
Reality comes closer when the speaker recognizes that
"All finite things reveal infinitude" and experiences
the eternal now-moment. This happens only when one
thinks by feeling, permitting the self to penetrate the
natural world. A belief quoted by Roethke in the
notebooks, in this instance without indicating the
author, states succinctly the spiritual reward of the
illuminated vision: "'He who sees the infinite in all
things, see God. He who sees the ratio only, sees
himself only'" (8 #112; 15 #220). Through the "rose in
the sea-wind" offered at the earthly level, the speaker
of the "North American Sequence" transcends the surface
self and partakes of the nature of Pure Being, creating
a new state of being--"A body with the motion of a
soul" (CP 188).

This rose is akin to the Imaginary Vision of which
Underhill speaks. Produced by "'that inward eye which
is the bliss of solitude,'" it is "an accommodation of
the supra-sensible to our human disabilities, a
symbolic reconstruction of reality on levels accessible
to sense" (M 285, 287). Though the speaker is
contemplating an actual rose, the self is aware that it
is being shown the truth in symbolic form. "Imaginary
Vision is the spontaneous and automatic activity of a
power which all artists, all imaginative people,
possess" Underhill maintains (M 285). Thus, the rose
which the poet has created through memory and
imagination is apprehended intuitively by the
speaker. Like the old woman, he has been given a

foretaste of the unitive Life. He has come "'to know
the hidden unity in the Eternal Being,'" a
characteristic perception of the Illuminative Way
(M 258).

Roethke has employed themes from mystical
literature in writing the "North American Sequence,"
most notably the emergence of the transcendent self
into the speaker's consciousness and the reconciliation
of opposites. In analyzing the characteristics of
mysticism, Underhill emphasizes that "its aims are
wholly transcendent and spiritual"; it focuses on union
with "a changeless One" who is "a living and personal
Object of love"; and it involves "an arduous
psychological and spiritual process"--the five steps of
the Mystic Way--"entailing the complete remaking of
character and the liberation of a new, or rather
latent, form of consciousness: (M 81). The "full
spiritual consciousness of the true mystic," she notes,
incorporates not only a sacramental view of the "active
World of Becoming" but also, more importantly, the
"power of apprehending the Absolute, Pure Being, the
utterly Transcendent" and thus experiencing "'passive
union with God'" (M 35-36). Roethke's speaker has
released the eternal child and has experienced unity of
being by perceiving Pure Being, not by achieving union
with It. The rose is a concrete symbol through which
he has received a message of perfection, not the Being
of Reality in which he has participated.

Ultimately, Underhill says, the person who
experiences this evolution of consciousness comes to
"transcendent point of view": he resolves "the paradox
of Being and Becoming" and knows the "unity in
diversity," the stillness in strife" (M 37). The
mystic is able to reconcile these opposites, Dean Inge

writes, because he realizes "in thought and feeling, the immanence of the temporal in the eternal, and of the eternal in the temporal."[14] Clearly this is one of the primary concerns of the sequence. William James analyzes the process of reconciliation, calling it the central insight of the mystical experience:

> It is as if the opposites of the world, whose contradictoriness and conflict make all our difficulties and troubles, were melted into unity. Not only do they, as contrasted species, belong to one and the same genus, but <u>one of the species</u>, the nobler and better one, <u>is itself the genus, and so soaks up and absorbs its opposites into itself</u> [his italics].[15]

The keynote of Roethke's sequence, embodied in the revelation of the "rose in the sea-wind," rooted "where sea and fresh water meet," is the reconciliation of these opposites.

It should be noted, however, that the expansion and unification of the self is only one stage of the arduous journey toward the mystic's transcendent point of view. Conversion and purgation are required whereby the character is remade, responding in loving union to the call of the Absolute. As Underhill cautions, "a definite and personal relation must be set up between the self and the Absolute Life." "To be a spectator is not enough," she continues; "The awakened subject is not merely to perceive transcendent life, but to participate therein" (<u>M</u> 195). The emphasis of Roethke's "North American Sequence" is on unity of self, not on the participation of that self in Divine Reality. The harmony created by the rose is the fulfillment of an idea Roethke expresses in the notebooks: "Both inner and outer reality the same: the final secret" (8 #112). The "imperishable quiet at the heart of form," symbolized by the rose, is an inner unity corresponding to the order which the speaker discovers in the natural world. The created opposites come into place as the speaker begins to see the eternal in the temporal, transforming time into an eternal now-moment. Roethke's way, then, is not to transcend time and corporeality, but rather to employ the intuitive vision to attain unity of being.

"SEQUENCE, SOMETIMES METAPHYSICAL"

> And I look with a hunter's eye toward
> eternity.
>   --Roethke Notebooks (14 #200)
> Poetry: "Language in motion: language doing
> its dance."
>   --Roethke Notebooks (8 #112)

The general movement of Roethke's sequences prior to the "Sequence, Sometimes Metaphysical" has been toward selfhood, a progress which has entailed the resolution of spiritual crises. If we follow the spiritual journeys of the three speakers we can see the progressive growth of the self as well as the development of Roethke's poetry from the meditative state toward the contemplative consciousness. In one form or another, each speaker has moved from multiplicity to simplicity or "singleness," as Roethke puts it. A poetic idea which Roethke entered in a 1946 notebook explains the importance of unity and wholeness: "Singleness = Discovery of singleness in self is the same as a discovery of God in oneself" (6 #84). Roethke's poetry has progressed gradually toward the unity of being symbolized by the rose at the end of the "North American Sequence," an intuition which would have been impossible for the son to grasp. The son's struggle for self-identity may be viewed as the first phase of Roethke's poetry, a necessary prelude to the stretchings of the self engaged in by the other speakers. Employing Recollection or Meditation, the son grows from spiritual awareness toward Awakening. He apprehends nature as a symbol of an unseen reality and learns to accept the soul as one with body, the essence of being simple or plain. His "effort to be born, and later, to become something more" (SP 37) ends with the recognition of the self as a sexual being who possesses a soul, one who is both fire and light. This understanding prepares for the journey of the self undertaken by the old woman and the protagonist of the "North American Sequence."

In the second phase of the poetry, the old woman and Roethke's American explorer renew and re-create the self by using Recollection or Meditation, Interior Quiet or Simplicity, and Ordinary Contemplation. These mental processes and the powers of the soul assist them in attaining a heightened understanding of the World of Becoming and achieving a sense of wholeness. By practicing Meditation and sinking into Quiet they have experienced Illumination of the Self. For the old woman this means she is released from her anxiety over non-being by a spiritual agent outside the self and learns of the eternal nature of the soul. For the protagonist of the "North American Sequence" this means establishing the self as a moving stillness amid the multiplicity or chaos of modern American life. In each instance, the speaker fulfills a definition of art expressed by Roethke in a 1949 notebook: "Art: To maintain self against the disruptive whole" (8 #110).

Their endeavor to attain simplicity of being has involved a journey of the self composed of several stages. Both speakers have looked inward to discern their spiritual malaise, awakened the inner self, come to know the self as the soul, and stretched beyond the self to apprehend the Eternal in the natural world and to achieve spiritual renewal. This inward and outward movement illustrates a fundamental principle which Roethke stated in a 1951 notebook: "Religion involves: Both moods of contraction and expansion of his being" (8 #116). Through a process of expansion and simplification, each has reached the stage of Interior Quiet, thus having enjoyed Awakening, Purification and Illumination of the Self. Their growth into higher realities reflects the progress outlined in Roethke's 1951 notebooks: "(1) Concentration, (2) Meditation, (3) Contemplation" (9 #121). The word Contemplation must be explained and qualified, however. By employing Ordinary or Natural Contemplation both protagonists have attained the Illuminative Vision. That is, they have experienced what Underhill calls in Practical Mysticism the "first form of contemplation": they have surrendered themselves to the message of the Eternal in the World of Becoming.[1] However, they have not undergone a deepening and widening of contemplation, lifting them into the higher forms of contemplation which produce the Dark Night of the Soul and Passive Union. A movement from "active" to "infused" contemplation is essential if Union with Divine Reality is to occur. Dean Inge speaks of this final stage as the "state of perfect contemplation."[2]

Now that the striving toward selfhood and unity of being has been fulfilled, Roethke's poetry evolves beyond the states of Recollection and Quiet to consider the state of Contemplation. A complementary urge initiates Roethke's final meditative sequence. Reaching beyond selfhood, Roethke's hero pushes toward a sense of union with God, descending finally into an experience of the harmony of the created universe. But Roethke's protagonists are perpetual beginners in constant search of the true self. In stretching the soul toward eternity the speaker of "Sequence,

Sometimes   Metaphysical"   attains   unity   of   being.
Roethke's understanding of the role of Contemplation in
the development of the mystic consciousness is found in
a 1957-58 notebook. As one might expect, it appears in
the form of notes from Underhill's <u>Mysticism</u>:

> Contemplation: The results & rewards of
>   Recollection and Quiet
> Contemplation: Thought, Love and Will become
>   a Unity
>
> . . .
>
> Contemplation is not, like meditation, one
>   simple state.
> A. Mystic's experience of Contemplation is
>   the experience of the All. This is <u>given</u>
>   not attained: Absolute revealed to him.
> B. This revealed Reality is apprehended by
>   way of participation, not by way of
>   observation (12 #174; Cf. <u>M</u> 328-29,
>   332-33).

The fact that these distinctions are recorded in the
notebooks does not necessarily mean that they will be
revealed in the poetry, of course. The study of
mysticism and the writing of poetry are clearly two
different activities. For example, Roethke may state
an explanation of the meaning of Union in the
notebooks--"'My being is God, not by simple
participation but by a true transformation of my
being'" (13 #188)--but his speaker in the "Sequence,
Sometimes Metaphysical" is unable to surrender the self
to receive this transformation.

One idea which Roethke gleaned from Underhill is,
nevertheless, important to consider as a framework for
an analysis of the last phase of the poetry.
Contemplation is a complex state involving several

degrees or stages, but it is ultimately a mode of consciousness through which one participates in rather than observes Reality. Whereas in Meditation one deliberately considers the "World of Becoming," perceiving Reality through a symbol, in Contemplation one surrenders the self and melts into the All, thus participating in revealed Reality. Further distinctions drawn by Underhill are not evident in Roethke's notes, however. The stage during which "thought, love, and will become a Unity" is called "contemplation proper" (M 329), and thus appears to be what she refers to in Practical Mysticism as "the second form of contemplation," that Divine Dark through which one approaches the "World of Being" (PM 120). Later she differentiates the "third form of contemplation" as the soul's experience of a "profound Quiet" during which the self merges with the Infinite Life of Absolute Reality. This final stage marks the change from "active" to "infused" Contemplation (PM 123).

"The Abyss" from the "Mixed Sequence" and the whole of the "Sequence, Sometimes Metaphysical" reflect the movement from terror to joy implied in Roethke's statement that his poems are "written out of passion, out of suffering--a suffering, mind you, transcended" (13 #186). He describes the "Sequence, Sometimes Metaphysical" as

> part of a search for God. They begin in
> terror at the abyss, at the edge of being,
> and descend, finally, into a more human, a
> more realizable condition. They turn away
> from loneliness and bleakness of metaphysical
> speculation to a shared love (13 #192).

"The Abyss" serves as a prelude to Roethke's search for
God in his final sequence. It, too, begins at the
abyss and moves toward a sense of union with God which
prepares for the cosmic Dance at the end of the
Sequence, one in which the speaker's "true self"
participates, experiencing the Divine Unity of
creation. With one eye looking toward eternity and the
other toward the natural world and human relationships,
Roethke's speaker journeys out of the self in search of
the Unknown God, the "wholly other" of which Rudolf
Otto speaks in The Idea of the Holy that fills the mind
with an overpowering sense of wonder and awe or dread.[3]

One way of approaching Absolute Reality, the
"Mysterium tremendum" that is "far removed," is to
"taste both the ground and the abyss" (10 #141), the
ground of the soul and the unfathomable abyss which is
the ground of Being. For Roethke, such an experience
involves "terror, anxiety, and fear"; "There is much to
be learned and wrung" from these states, he says:
"there are still 'forms' which the imagination can
seize from these dark areas of the mind and spirit"
(9 #123). "The Abyss" dramatizes the truth of this
statement. At the same time it embodies the speaker's
intense, desperate struggle to transcend the mental and
spiritual terror associated with the abyss and to
attain the contemplative mode of being. The movement
of "The Abyss" from disintegration of the self to
wholeness of being can only be understood
intuitively. Since it dramatizes a mystical experience
which is ineffable, the poem does not proceed
rationally. It is a loosely constructed meditation
which culminates in the speaker's communion with God.[4]

In the opening section, Roethke seems to be
portraying not only the speaker's psychic disorder but

also Jacob Boehme's _Ungrund_, "the dark and irrational abyss that precedes being."[5] The meditation begins with the prelude, "composition of place," in which the divided self contemplates the dark stair descending into the abyss:

> Is the stair here?
> Where's the stair?
> 'The stair's right there,
> But it goes nowhere.'
>
> And the abyss? The abyss?
> 'The abyss you can't miss:
> It's right where you are--
> A step down the stair' (_CP_ 219).

The speaker stands precariously at the edge of the stair, fearful of the darkness, but he must descend, for this is the dark nothingness which is also the source of light. By climbing down the stair, he will be lifted to the Divine darkness of Absolute Reality. The extent of the speaker's psychological and spiritual decay is depicted in the next stanzas. Language and rhythms break down, communicating a sense of emptiness and futility. The continuous return of failure to "Part of a house" indicates his inner division, the separation of body and soul. There is no spiritual progress, for he lacks desire: "The wind's slowing," he says (_CP_ 219). With the disintegration of thought and will, it is not surprising that the poet omits the Ignatian second prelude in which the meditator asks God for what he desires to achieve in the meditation. Instead, the speaker descends into a purgative state of self-examination.

In Section 2, then, he acknowledges his dead spiritual life:

I have been spoken to variously
But heard little.
My inward witness is dismayed
By my unguarded mouth.
I have taken, too often, the dangerous path,
The vague, the arid,
Neither in nor out of this life (CP 220).

The inner self is appalled by the speaker's dry, false existence, his lack of commitment and purpose in attaining true being. He hears "the noise of the wall," the voices of "Those who despise the dove" of peace, of the Holy Ghost (CP 220). These are the babbling tongues of the world that invade the speaker in the third stanza. He calls upon "Whitman, maker of catalogues" to strengthen him against the power of these voices and "the terrible hunger for objects" that makes him quail (CP 220). We make a "fetish of 'thing-hood,'" Roethke comments in "On Identity'": 'we surround ourselves with junk, ugly objects . . ." (CP 19-20). Whitman, the cataloguer and visionary poet, will help him control and transcend this invasion of the material world. But the journey toward being requires more than the protection of Whitman: it demands a metamorphosis, a transformation of the self. Roethke quotes from Dean Inge: "We must die to our lower self not once only, but continually, so that we may rise in stepping stones of our dead selves to higher things" (12 #172). It is appropriate, then, that the speaker selects the caterpillar for his symbol. As the caterpillar suffers the darkness of the cocoon to emerge as a butterfly, so he must undergo the darkness of the abyss to become a spiritual man. Like the caterpillar, he has "moved closer to death, lived with death" (CP 220). This "sly surly attendant" has

watched him for weeks. He still wonders "Who sent him
away?" (CP 220). The crisis has passed, but the poet's
night journey is just beginning. "From me to Thee's a
long and terrible way," Roethke says in "The Marrow"
(CP 246). Thus the speaker is "no longer a bird
dipping a beak into rippling water"; he has become "a
mole winding through earth, / A night-fishing otter,"
one who hunts for its food in the dark (CP 220). These
are apt symbols of the self as it moves toward the life
of the spirit. As Meister Eckhart says, "Covertly,
nature seeks, hunts, tries to ferret out the track on
which God may be found."[6]

The speaker's "painful descent into the 'cell of
self-knowledge'" (M 233) is followed in Section 3 by an
analytical discourse in which the self comes to a new
understanding about the nature of the abyss. In an
effort to describe the threatening presence of the
abyss, Roethke employs a Homeric simile. He compares
the "blinding misery" of the abyss--that "terrible
violence of creation"--with the "cold fire" that seems
to strike when "smells" rush out from "a florist's
storeroom" (CP 220-21). Through oxymoron he creates
the paradoxical nature of each experience. The effect
of each is the same, however: "Too much reality can be
a dazzle, a surfeit; / Too close immediacy an
exhaustion" (CP 220). A prose version of the first
stanza, found in Roethke's notebooks, clearly indicates
that the word "reality" refers to the natural world,
not Absolute Reality, as William Heyen contends:[7]

> He who is most aware of his immediate
> surroundings may also be seized most
> intensely by the longing to fly away, to
> escape them. For too close immediacy can

bring exhaustion, too much beauty is a
dazzle, a surfeit . . . (11 #152).
As beauty can be "a dazzle, a surfeit," so it is with
the abyss, the "flash into the burning heart of the
abominable" (CP 221). But instead of escaping this
cold fire, the speaker descends into a state of
waiting, an expectant calm in which his fear subsides
and he is filled with the active passivity peculiar to
the mystics:

> Yet if we wait, unafraid, beyond the fearful
>   instant,
> The burning lake turns into a forest pool,
> The fire subsides into rings of water,
> A sunlit silence (CP 221).

This intuition of the fire becoming water is the
turning point in the meditation, the first hint of the
speaker's spiritual awakening. In this instance, then,
the steps of the Mystic Way are reversed, with
Purgation preceding Awakening. The narrator has not
yet attained the Illumination of the Self that
William Heyen urges.[8] Instead, he waits courageously,
"beyond the fearful instant" and experiences a moment
of quiet in which the Eternal penetrates the temporal,
creating the Eternal Now. In this moment which is both
in and out of time, opposites come into place and he
apprehends the nature of the abyss. As he returned
from the cold of the florist's storeroom "the heat of
August, / Chastened," so he returns from the "slippery
cold heights" of the abyss to stillness and light
(CP 220-21). The abyss may hold the threat of non-
being, but it is also the source of light, "A sunlit
silence."

Section 4 of "The Abyss" is the speaker's central
discourse, a colloquy with the self which exhibits his

growth in the life of the spirit. "Progress in
contemplation," Underhill explains, is characterized by
"an alternation of light and shade: at first between
consolation' and aridity'; then between dark
contemplation' and sharp intuitions of Reality"
(M 383). Roethke's protagonist withstands these mental
and spiritual oscillations, rocking or shifting between
states of doubt and illumination. Though Heyen
presents a reasonable argument, I am not convinced that
this colloquy embodies the Dark Night of the Soul.[9]
Underhill insists that the Dark Night "must entail
bitter suffering: far worse than that endured in the
Purgative Way," but Roethke's speaker does not
experience such intense pain (M 389). Furthermore, the
various forms which this "great negation" may assume
are not found in the speaker's discourse: the feeling
that God has "deliberately withdrawn His Presence,
never, perhaps, to manifest Himself again" (M 389);
the "black 'conviction of sin'" (M 390); "complete
emotional lassitude" (M 392); a "dark ecstasy or 'pain
of God,'" the "abrupt invasion of a wild and
unendurable desire to 'see God,' apprehend the
Transcendent in its fullness: which can only, they
think, be satisfied by death" (M 394). This "mystic
death" is the final purification of the will, the
annihilation of selfhood that prepares for the Unitive
Life. Instead of undergoing this Dark Night, Roethke's
speaker experiences progress in contemplation, moving
through the Cloud of Unknowing to the moment of
Illumination.[10] Thus, I cannot agree with Neil Bowers'
interpretation that the entire poem focuses on the
mystic death, for this is the most intense period of
the Dark Night of the Soul.[11] Roethke's speaker

foregoes the great negation in which the self is annihilated in preparation for union. Instead, he assumes an attitude of not-knowing and expresses the fulfillment of union.

The opening stanza of Section 4 clearly indicates the narrator's renewed desire. He longs to reach beyond this world, but can he "outleap the sea-- / The edge of all the land, the final sea?" (CP 221). He envies "the tendrils, their eyeless seeking," for they stretch beyond themselves unhampered by the "I," the ego (CP 221). Submitting his will to "the wind," symbolic of the spirit and the awakening of desire, he comes "home from the spirit and the awakening of desire, he comes "home from the twilight and fishing" (CP 221). This submission creates the speaker's condition of "half-rest" in which he enters the Cloud of Unknowing:

> In this, my half-rest,
> Knowing slows for a moment,
> And not-knowing enters, silent,
> Bearing being itself,
> And the fire dances
> To the stream's
> Flowing (CP 221).

When "not-knowing enters" the speaker plunges himself into darkness by renouncing all the discursive workings of the mind. This state of ignorance is paradoxically the most perfect way of knowing the Absolute--the Mysterium tremendum et fascinans[12]--for he who knows nothing of the mind and the understanding knows everything of the heart, intuitively. "We come to something without knowing why," Roethke says in "The Manifestation" (CP 235). "The knowledge of the cloud," as William Johnston has noted, is "dark,

supraconceptual, contemplative, mystical."[13]   It is
"dark wisdom, grounded on faith and produced by love"
[his italics].[14]   As Hugh of St. Victor testifies,
"Love knocks and enters but knowledge stands without"
(8 #112). Roethke quotes this passage from The Cloud
of Unknowing in his notebooks: "Saint Denis, 'The most
goodly knowing of God is that which is known by
unknowing.'--the way of ignorance" (11 #147).[15] Later
in the notebooks Roethke comments: "What is there to
know? Not-knowing. . . . We think by feeling. What
is there to know?   The answer is un-knowing--the
unknowing of the cloud of un-knowing" (14 #208). When
not-knowing enters it bears "being itself," and
opposites are reconciled: fire and water become one.

In her investigation of the ways in which
contemplatives perceive of the Absolute, Underhill
finds that the Godhead is described in two different
ways in mystical literature, corresponding to the
direction in which the mystic consciousness has
extended. Those who contemplate Divine Transcendence
speak of God as "the Unconditioned, the Wholly Other
for whom we have no words. . . . To see Him is to
enter the Darkness, the 'Cloud of Unknowing,' and 'know
only that we know nought'" (M 337). When they attempt
to express the nature of this contemplative life, they
"adopt the Dionysian concept of Divine Darkness, or the
parallel idea of the fathomless Abyss, the Desert of
the Godhead, the Eckhartian 'still wilderness where no
one is at home'" (M 338). The speaker of "The Abyss"
is clearly this type of self rather than one who
contemplates God immanent in the soul and speaks of the
loving communion as a Marriage with Uncreated Light
that creates a state of Being (M 342).

Roethke's speaker has glimpsed the harmony of
"being itself," but in stanza three he becomes the prey
of his own shifting mental and spiritual states and is
overcome by doubt: "Do we move toward God, or merely
another condition?" (CP 221). Soon he hears "a river's
undersong" which leads him to a state of Quiet that
provides its own answer to his desperate question. "I
rock between dark and dark," he says, between the
darkness of doubt and the dark contemplation of
mystical illumination.   As he climbs toward the
Absolute, his "dead selves" sing, ushering in a new
state of calm (CP 221). Contemplation deepens and the
speaker reaches a profound Quiet by penetrating under
the leaves to the ground of created nature:

> Such quiet under the small leaves!--
> Near the stem, whiter at root,
> A luminous stillness
>
> (CP 221)

The metaphysical overtones are unmistakable. Roethke's
speaker seems to have touched that "luminous stillness"
which is the root or origin of life, the Ground of
Being itself--a darkness which is its own light. By
tasting the ground, he has approached the Truth which
Dionysius the Areopagite says is "hidden in the
dazzling obscurity of the secret Silence, outshining
all brilliance with the intensity of [its]
darkness."[16] "'Who knows this-- / Knows all,'" the
shade says: "'Adore and draw near'" (CP 222). "'Be
still, be still, and know,'" Underhill observes, "is
the condition of man's purest and most direct
apprehensions of reality: and he experiences in quiet
the truest and deepest activity . . . [her italics]" (M
38). The speaker has drawn near "the 'ground': the

eternal original unity" (9 #124). This intuition
prepares him for the final revelation.

In Section 5 of "The Abyss" the speaker's desire
is fulfilled: he experiences communion with God. The
intensity of his need and the constancy of his vigil
are expressed in his declaration that he has thirsted
and watched for the Eternal throughout the day and the
night. His obedience and love are now rewarded: "I
receive! I have been received!" he proclaims
(CP 222). Suddenly his perception of the natural world
is sharpened and he hears "the flowers drinking in
their light" (CP 222). Once again he acknowledges that
"the soft-backed creatures"--"the crab and the sea
urchin"--have been his teachers (CP 149, 222).
Recalling his own spiritual journey, he meditates upon
the movement of "small waters":

> I recall the falling of small waters,
> The stream slipping beneath the mossy logs,
> Winding down to the stretch of irregular
> sand,
> The great logs piled like matchsticks
> (CP 222).

In tones of humility and awe the speaker announces his
"Spiritual Marriage":

> I am most immoderately married:
> The Lord God has taken my heaviness away;
> I have merged, like the bird, with the bright
> air,
> And my thought flies to the place by the bo-
> tree.
> Being, not doing, is my first joy (CP 222).

Now Roethke's protagonist employs the language of the
contemplative "for whom intimate and personal communion
has been the mode under which he best apprehended

Reality," one who "speaks of the consummation of this
communion, its perfect and permanent form, as the
Spiritual Marriage of his soul with God" [her italics]
(M 415). He is "immoderately married," for the union
is beyond all rational understanding. "The Lord God
has taken my heaviness away," he says. He is no longer
the caterpillar crawling down the string toward
death. A double union is implied in these lines: a
higher and lower merging of the self and a union in
which the knower and the known are one. Underhill
stresses that to the mystics of the "intimate" type
"the Unitive Life has meant not self-loss in an
Essence, but self-fulfillment in the union of heart and
will" (M 426). An indication of this fulfillment is
the joy that the speaker expresses when he experiences
the contemplative state of being. In this moment when
the spiritual life is achieved, Underhill says, "The
contemplative is merged in it 'like a bird in the air,
like a fish in the sea': loses to find and dies to
live" (M 333; Cf. 13 #176). Whereas in the "North
American Sequence" the protagonist became "A body with
the motion of a soul," the speaker of "The Abyss" seems
to experience a mind/body split. His thought flies to
the place by the bo-tree," the place of perfection and
illuminated knowledge. However, since Being is known
passively through the mind or spirit, not through the
motion of the body, the implied separation is only an
appearance of the true experience. Though Roethke
comments in a 1962 notebook that "Like St. Theresa, I
cannot distinguish between the terms body, mind, and
spirit" (15 #210), the important point is that the
value and nature of the contemplative life can only be
communicated by those who, "in the metaphor of
Plotinus," have "'taken flight towards the Thought of

God'" (M 335).   Such flight results in the speaker's
final illumination.

The final line of the poem--"Being, not doing, is
my first joy"--is set off from the rest of the text as
a statement of the effect of the meditative process
upon the speaker.   It indicates what he has brought
back with him from his descent into the abyss.   The
echo of Underhill is, of course, unmistakable: "Being,
not Doing, is the first aim of the mystic . . ."
(M 380).   The word "being," as used by the mystics,
refers to the Being of God and to the moment of the
Eternal Birth when, through the birth of God in the
apex of the soul, one truly is.   Roethke quotes this
passage in the notebooks, in this instance without
indicating his source:

> 'Indeed God Himself does not rest there where
> he is merely the first beginning of being.
> Rather, He rests there where He is the end
> and the goal of all being.   Not that being
> comes to nought there; rather it becomes
> perfected there to its highest perfection'
>   (14 #206).

"Only Being can know Being," Underhill testifies: "we
'behold that which we are, and are that which we
behold'" (M 41).   Thus Roethke's speaker is affirming
his joyful, free participation in Eternal Life, the
essence of the Unitive State.   Although Roethke admits
in "On 'Identity'" that he never experienced the
mystical union of God with the soul, he has
communicated through the speaker of "The Abyss" not
only the possibility of communion with God but also the
consummation of the Unitive Life.   "I can't claim that
the soul, my soul, was absorbed in God," Roethke
said.   "No, God for me still remains someone to be

confronted, to be dueled with" (SP 26). It may be
unjust to Roethke to end with this statement, for in
the notebooks he expresses emotions which reach beyond
the idea of contending with God. In the late 1940's or
early 1950's he commented, "Because I duel with God is
no sign I don't love Him" (10 #135), while in a 1961-62
entry he stated, "If I am not humble before God, I am
humble before what has been said about a duel with God"
(14 #200). Roethke's contest with God is a struggle
which is augmented by humility and love. It is this
ensemble of emotions that drives the poet and his
speakers from multiplicity to unity of being, from
self-involvement to the Unknown God. This desire to
encounter God precipitates the journey undertaken in
the "Sequence, Sometimes Metaphysical," a movement
which Roethke describes as "a hunt, a drive toward
God."[17]

II

In Roethke's poetry there is no division between
the self and the natural world, no separation between
God and His creation. But there is an abyss between
God and the self or soul. In an effort to span the
distance and "to come as close to God as possible,"
Roethke wrote the "Sequence, Sometimes Metaphysical
(DT 49). That hunt for God is reflected throughout the
notebooks in the form of a wrestle with God and what
appears to be a struggle for belief. Only a few
scholars have commented on Roethke's belief in God,
primarily in an effort to determine the nature of the
God in whom he believed, if indeed he held any
belief. I do not pretend to offer any startling
insights; rather I propose to let Roethke speak for
himself. His words testify to his growth in belief.

Roethke began educating himself in the contemplative life in the late 1930's and the early 1940's, but doubt remained. During these years he groped for belief in God and was haunted by the figure of Jesus Christ whom he considered to be feminine. "I don't believe there is a God," he says in an early entry, "but to try to believe is one of the noblest human efforts" (4 #53). "That I am one of a company of men who did believe in God--that is enough, I think," he notes in 1948 or 1949 (8 #107). But apparently it was not enough, for he tries desperately to regain his belief. "We live by fictions and myths," he writes at one point. "If there is no God, we invent one etc." (5 #61). Richard Blessing contends that he did invent a God "according to his need, a God especially for poets; and, having created God, the poet began to live by Him and found Him, at least on occasion, to be there."[18]   I would claim, on the other hand, that Roethke came to a true belief in God the creator. The belief that overcame him apparently grew out of his need for God and his anxiety over God's absence. "How terrible the need for God," he exclaims in a 1944-45 notebook (5 #68). Earlier that year he makes a notation that indicates the sense of God's absence and implies his consternation over the theology of the Trinity:

Wait. Watch. Listen. Meditate. He'll come. When? No, I know He won't come. He doesn't care about me any more. No, I mean Him, the Big He, that big three-cornered Papa (5 #66).

His sense of alienation and his desire to confront God are expressed in a 1947-49 entry when he speaks of himself as a man who "duels with God" and is "given no

sign" (7 #135). By 1945-46 he had apparently begun to
recognize the necessity of loving God:

> Early state: Why should God be loved: why
> does he need loving? But then I became aware
> of a truth: that he doesn't need or demand
> the love except as I need it. It is
> necessary for me to love God for my own
> salvation if for no other reason than to
> escape from the love of mere man or nature
>   (6 #77).

Roethke continues to read mystical literature,
meditating upon whether "God is the point in the
deepest self?" (6 #88), and gradually belief overtakes
him. This comment in a 1949-50 notebook is, in my
view, one of the most revealing entries from these
early years:

> I remember telling Burke that I was saving
> for my old age two things: the belief in God
> and a consideration of abstract thought.
> Both are beginning, and there's no alas in me
>   (8 #113).

Belief may have entered the mind, but it did not bring
Roethke a sense of the immanence of God. Instead, he
began to consider the immortality or survival of man.
As this 1949-51 entry states, God remained an "amiable
opponent," though not totally absent from this life:

> In my own case, the first powerful intuitive
> conviction came, not of the presence of God,
> but of one's own survival: "we don't die."
> But God remains a kind of amiable opponent:
> on your side, almost outside this life (9 #123).

The closest Roethke comes to an affirmation of belief
during these years is a statement dated 1951-52,
suggesting that he considers God the creator: "If God

does not exist, neither do we" (9 #120). Apparently he began to feel the presence of God, for in 1961 he asserts that "God is not far away. He has been put aside, ignored, not seen by the egomaniacal 'thinkers'" (14 #200). Roethke's renewal of belief and this intuition of the immanent God did not precipitate his return to organized religion, however. His denial of theological systems is stressed in this 1960 entry:

> I'm aware that among the expert (unfrightened!) trans-Atlantic literary theologians that to approach God without benefit of clergy is a grievous lapse in taste, if not a mortal sin. But in crawling out of a swamp, or up what small rock-faces I try to assay, I don't need a system on my back (14 #194).

Roethke does not need a system, for he now believes that God is accessible in this world. In February of 1963, he states his conviction in "On Identity'" that "there is a God, and He's here, immediate, accessible" (SP 27).

The deity in whom Roethke finally came to believe is a God who is both transcendent and immanent in the world. In "On 'Identity'" he quotes St. Thomas Aquinas in explaining why he calls on "all living things, including the sub-human":[19]

> Everything that lives is holy: I call upon these holy forms of life. One could even put this theologically: St. Thomas says, "God is above all things by the excellence of his nature; nevertheless, He is in all things as causing the being of all things." Therefore, in calling upon the snail, I am calling, in a sense, upon God (SP 24-25).

Later in the essay Roethke affirms the various ways in
which God's presence may be felt in the world:

> He is equally accessible now, not only in
> works of art or in the glories of a
> particular religious service, or in the
> light, the aftermath that follows the dark
> night of the soul, but in the lowest forms of
> life, He moves and has His being. Nobody has
> killed off the snails (SP 27).

For Roethke, God is immanent in the universe, a
spiritual reality supporting and conditioning all
things, a God of panentheism: not that everything is
God, but that God is in everything. Even the stones
are permeated with Being. Roethke quotes Angela of
Foligno: "'The whole world is impregnated with God'"
(8 #117). But Roethke's God is also transcendent, as
the passage from St. Thomas indicates. The "spirit /
Or agency" that touches the old woman in "Meditations,"
the "Lord God" who takes away the speaker's "heaviness"
in "The Abyss," and the God who enters "the mind" in
"In a Dark Time" is a transcendent God becoming
immanent. Roethke comments in the notebooks, echoing
Meister Eckhart, "As soon as you are ready, God will
pour himself into you" (6 #193).[20]

Vincent Buckley misses the mark, then, when he
asserts that Roethke is "a poet of the purely immanent
God, if of any".[21] I would argue, to the contrary,
that Roethke is a panentheist. Roethke records Dean
Inge's definition of panentheism in the notebooks:
"the belief in the immanence of a God who is also
transcendent" (15 #218).[22] For Roethke, as for Rudolf
Otto, God is not "wholly 'wholly other'" [his
italics].[23] The God who appears near the end of "In a
Dark Time" seems to be more abstract and more totally

transcendent than the spirit that generates the old woman's rebirth, but as Roethke admits, "Sequence, Sometimes Metaphysical" begins in the "loneliness and bleakness of metaphysical speculation" (13 #192). Ultimately, Roethke's God is more often immanent in the natural world than in the mind or soul. Thus a "drive toward God" is necessary if Roethke is to feel the presence of God more closely (DT 49).

III

"Sequence, Sometimes Metaphysical" is a meditation which Roethke described as "an effort to break through the barrier of rational experience" into the World of Being (DT 49). It begins in dark contemplation at the edge of being and descends finally into a cosmic dance in which flesh and spirit, known and Unknown are one. The eye that "begins to see" in the darkness and uncertainty of the opening poems (CP 239) becomes "the Eye altering all" at the end of the sequence (CP 251). The speaker who cries out in despair, "Which I is I?" (CP 239), surrenders his will "Till mystery is no more" (CP 250) and finds the "true self" (CP 251). Once again the way down is the way up. Through the "Death of the self in a long, tearless night" the transcendental self emerges and Roethke's speaker participates in the oneness of the universe (CP 239).

"In a Dark Time" is an opening prelude which establishes the subject and the place of Roethke's meditative sequence. It depicts an attempt "to break from the bondage of the self, from the barriers of the 'real' world to come as close to God as possible" (DT 49). "One begins in this dark time," Roethke comments in the notebooks. "How did one get there? I think every human knows, not merely the technically

manic-depressed" (14 #194). But this dark goes beyond
the "self-created dark" of psychic confusion mentioned
by Roethke (DT 49). It also represents a spiritual
despair, a dark night of the soul which the speaker
consciously risks in order to reach God. St. John of
the Cross characterizes the Dark Night as a sense of
the absence of God:

> When this purgative contemplation oppresses a
> man, he feels very vividly indeed the shadow
> of death, the sighs of death, and the sorrows
> of hell, all of which reflect the feeling of
> God's absence, of being chastised and
> rejected by Him, and of being unworthy of
> Him, as well as the object of His anger. The
> soul experiences all this and even more, for
> now it seems that this afflication will last
> forever.[24]

Sinking into this purgative contemplation, the speaker
experiences sharp oscillations of darkness and light,
characteristic of the stress and tribulation of the
Dark Night. As he deepens in contemplation, God enters
the mind and the speaker is rapt out of himself into
the freedom of the One. Although I recognize that "In
a Dark Time" may be interpreted according to the
ascending steps of the Mystic Way, as Neal Bowers has
done,[25] I think the poem is more appropriately viewed
as a dramatization of Roethke's conviction that
"Despair and the most transcendental love of God are
inseparable" (SF 190). In the poem this belief is
transformed into the dramatic movement of the self into
new levels of contemplation, leading him out of the
Dark Night to a sense of Union which appears to be a
state of Rapture.

In the first two stanzas of "In a Dark time" Roethke creates the journey of "the edge" through the use of "composition of place" and painful self-analysis. The opening lines establish the poem's central paradox and the speaker's consciousness of mortality:

> In a dark time, the eye begins to see,
> I meet my shadow in the deepening shade;
> I hear my echo in the echoing wood--
>   (CP 239).

In his exalted meditative state the speaker's sense perceptions are increased, suggesting the beginning of his movement from ignorance to knowledge of the self. He sees his other self and hears his echo. This dark wood reverberating with sound is a psychological and spiritual hell in which the speaker meets his shadow, "my double, my Other, usually tied to me, my reminder that I am going to die . . ." (DT 50). Knowing that he must die, he weeps. As Roethke puts it, the speaker is aware "of the human condition that has not, as yet, been transcended" (DT 50). Implied in this statement is a further recognition that the "I," the ego--the surface self--must be transcended before he will see clearly and thus achieve true identity. "I live between the heron and the wren," he says, "Beasts of the hill and serpents of the den" (CP 239). His identity swings from one to the other as he calls "upon their powers," their wisdom and courage, to protect and guide him in his "spiritual ascent or assault" (DT 51). In stanza two the mind begins to burn with illumination: "The day's on fire!" (CP 239). This state of dark revelation causes him to "know the purity of pure despair," the distance between the self and God. He sees the Other "pinned against a sweating

wall" (CP 239), while "The true self still maintains
its choice, its mobility" (DT 51). For the moment, at
least, the way out of despair is neither the "cave" nor
the "winding path": "The edge is what I have," he says
(CP 239). The speaker lives on "the edge" of being,
rocking   between   despair   and   illumination,   ever
conscious of "the terrible abyss" that separates him
from God (DT 51). His journey of the edge will either
come to a dead-end or will demonstrate "How body from
spirit slowly does unwind / Until we are pure spirit at
the end" (CP 244).

In the third stanza the speaker proclaims that "A
steady storm of correspondences!" is breaking in upon
the mind (CP 239). Like Swedenborg and Blake, he is
being bombarded by a stream of analogies between "the
real and unseen world, and the illusory manifestations
which we call the world of sense" (M 160). These
signs--"A night flowing with birds, a ragged moon, /
And in broad day the midnight come again!"--storm his
consciousness, reminding him of the divine world
(CP 239). This "storm of correspondences" is so
overwhelming that the speaker loses all sense of
time: day and night are reversed. The overpowering
sense of the immediacy of the invisible world provokes
a change:

A man goes far to find out what he is--
Death of the self is a long, tearless night,
All natural shapes blazing unnatural light

(CP 239).

Everything seems to be blazing with supernatural light,
especially the speaker's self. Underhill speaks of the
change in the "'natural' self" in her discussion of
purgation:

That which we call the 'natural' self as it
exists in the 'natural' world--the 'old Adam'
of St. Paul--is wholly incapable of super-
sensual adventure.   All its activites are
grouped about a centre of consciousness whose
correspondences   are   with   the   material
world. In the moment of its awakening, it is
abruptly made aware of this disability.   It
knows itself finite.   It now aspires to the
infinite (M 199).

In Roethke's poem the natural or phenomenal self is not
merely purified by "unnatural light"; it dies in the
blaze during a "long, tearless night."

The speaker is tossed back into darkness in stanza
four: "Dark my light, and darker my desire" (CP 239).
He perceives his soul to be "some heat-maddened summer
fly" that "Keeps buzzing at the sill," trying to get
out of his sense-laden body--to break its barriers
(CP 239). "Which I is I?" he cries out in the agony of
self-disgust (CP 239).   The intensity of the self's
identification with this mad insect marks the turning
point of the poem, the moment of crisis.   In the
notebooks Roethke observes that "The swing around from
terror--the dead emptiness of the soul--is quick and
complete or not at all" (14 #200).   Roethke expands
upon the nature of this change in his essay on the
poem:

The moment before Nothingness, before near-
annihilation, the moment of supreme disgust
is the worst: when change comes it is either
total loss of consciousness--symbolical or
literal death--or a quick break into another
state, not necessarily serene, but frequently

a   bright   blaze   of   consciousness   that
translates itself into action (DT 52).
Although the speaker is "A fallen man"--fallen from
grace and thrown into despair--his terrifying descent
into Nothingness halts.   Roethke   comments   in   the
notebooks, "I may be split, indecisive, divided, but I
am still a man, albeit fallen, and I return to the task
of climbing out of my fear" (14 #200).   Aided by the
will, the true self rises above the dead self and the
speaker in turn overcomes his fear of God.   This
deliberate act in which the surface self and its fear
have   been   annihilated   precipitates   the   speaker's
experience of union:

   The mind enters itself, and God the mind,
   And one is One, free in the tearing wind
                       (CP 239).

Roethke may have recalled a passage from Underhill
which he recorded in the notebooks.   In discussing the
practice of meditation, Underhill notes that all of
man's faculties contribute in producing this willed
state of consciousness.   By such meditation, says
Richard of St. Victor, "'God enters into the mind,' and
'the mind also enters into itself'" (M 315; 12 #172).
During meditation the mind has been beyond itself; now
it returns home, bringing God with it.   The mind turns
into itself and God enters also.   Unity is regained.
This act of meditation is "proper to one who has
attained the first degree of ardent love," Underhill
says (M 315).   This meditative act has clearly been
transformed in the final stanza of Roethke's poem.   It
now represents the second form of contemplation in
which "man's 'made Trinity' of thought, love, and will,
becomes a Unity" (M 329), catapulting the speaker into
the freedom of the Godhead.

In his explication of the poem's final line, "And one is One, free in the tearing wind," Roethke states that "the one not merely makes his peace with God" but "he--if we read One as the Godhead theologically placed above God--transcends God: he becomes the Godhead itself, not only the veritable creator of the universe but the creator of the revealed God" (DT 53). Roethke's distinction between God and the Godhead has obviously been influenced by his reading Tillich's The Courage to Be but it may also be related to Boehme's "divine Unground," the principle of freedom that exists in darkness before the trinity.[26]   Unlike Meister Eckhart, who speaks of the Godhead as a desert, empty of activity, where the soul may rest,[27] Roethke seems to perceive the Godhead as absolute freedom: "The protagonist one and/or the godhead are 'free' in the 'tearing wind'--free to be buffeted by their own creation" (DT 53). Roethke makes a significant comment in the notebooks which he chose not to include in his essay: "'The soul becomes God by participation'--in what?   In this welter of His created world, by which He Himself is buffeted" (14 #200). Perhaps he had second thoughts about the pantheistic implications of his statement.   Nevertheless, the important point is that this is one way, perhaps the only way, Roethke could imagine participation between the soul and God.   Though he quotes Meister Eckhart's analysis of the Eternal Birth in the notebooks, Roethke's antagonism toward Christ would have prevented him from believing in a participation whereby the soul is born again in God and the Father begets His Son in the soul.   For Eckhart, the birth of God in the soul is synonymous with mystic union: "he begets his Son in the core of the soul and is made One with it."[28]   But for Roethke, the soul

becomes God by participating "In this welter of His
created world." Roethke's protagonist "makes his peace
with God" and then leaps into the freedom of the
Godhead. Even though "God Himself, in his most supreme
manifestation, risks being maimed, if not destroyed" by
the buffeting wind, Roethke says he is comforted by the
hope "that some other form or aspect of God will endure
with man again, will save him from himself" (DT 53).
This hope is found in the pun on the word "tearing,"
which may mean ripping or crying. The ambiguity of the
word suggests "that the ambient air itself, that powers
man once deemed merely 'natural,' or is unaware of, are
capable of pity" (DT 53).

Yet the hope is faint and the violence of the
dramatic action remains. Roethke has explained that
the poem depicts an attempt to reach God by breaking
down the barriers of rational experience; a statement
which underscores the fact that this union is forced
rather than infused. The sense of union described in
"The Abyss," though it resounds with echoes of
Underhill's analysis, nevertheless represents a passive
not a violent union; the nature of which appears to be
more orthodox than the leap into the Godhead with the
possibility of God being destroyed. Perhaps the
crucial idea for Roethke is that the speaker makes
peace with God before the dramatic union with the
Godhead. Despite this comment, the pantheistic
implications of Roethke's analysis will be disturbing
to the orthodox, suggesting that God is confined in and
therefore buffeted by His creation: immanent but not
transcendant.

Roethke insisted that "In a Dark Time" was "a
dictated poem, something given, scarcely mine at all.
For about three days before its writing I felt

disembodied, out of time; then the poem virtually wrote itself, on a day in summer, 1958" (DT 49). In the notebooks he defines the "'dictated'" poem as the "swiftly written poem, the poem written in some crisis of the psyche" (10 #129). But the word "dictated" also suggests spiritual inspiration resulting from an "absorbed state of recollection in which the creative faculty works most freely" (M 294). The meditative state depicted in the poem seems to be related to the active imaginary vision described by Underhill. Roethke records her distinction between the passive and active visions in the notebooks: "Passive vision is the deeper self expressing itself; active vision is the result of a change in that deeper self—usually a crisis" (12 #172; cf. M 290). The dynamic vision of "In a Dark Time" is an "automatic expression of intense subliminal activity" which produces a change in the deeper self (M 290). The dramatic action envisioned in the final line of the poem—union with the Godhead—was so terrifying to Roethke that he admitted, "I wrote not a thing for three months after it" (14 #200). It may be a "cry from the mire" as Roethke stated, but it is also an outward sign of the movement of the speaker's self toward a new level of consciousness (DT 53). If the final lines of the poem are accepted on their own terms and Roethke's analysis ignored, the speaker's description of union may resemble Rapture. Underhill explains that the contemplative may experience the sense of rising into the freedom of the All abruptly; that is, it may seize the individual, manifesting itself in uncontrollable "psychic disturbances": "an indication of disharmony between the subject's psycho-physical make-up and his transcendental powers" (M 376). The mental and spiritual disorder of

Roethke's speaker as well as his sudden experience of union correspond to Underhill's analysis and may help explain the nature of Roethke's automatic imaginary vision.

The poems which follow "In a Dark Time" explore the problem of how one is to live in this world after the sense of transcendence has passed. Roethke's meditative sequence "turns away from loneliness and bleakness of metaphysical speculation," descending finally into "a shared love" (13 #192). Before Roethke's protagonist experiences the cosmic dance of the universe, he employs the powers of the soul-- memory, understanding and will--and a meditative process involving composition, analysis and colloquy to simplify the self until it is a pure soul, stretching it into pure being. The oscillations between doubt and illumination continue as he moves from fear and anxiety to freedom and joy. Descending the steps of the mystic way, he grows from Meditation into Quiet, sinking finally into Ordinary or Natural Contemplation.

"In Evening Air" is a second prelude in which Roethke's speaker petitions God for that which he desires to achieve in the meditation: "Make me, O Lord, at last, a simple thing / Time cannot overwhelm" (CP 240). This prayer for pure simplicity is a longing for self-simplification. As Roethke says in the notebooks, "Time, teach my flesh a way of being plain!" (15 #221). Being plain is to be at once single (whole) and naked. He must be purged of multiplicity, illusion and imperfection in order to become wholly bare:

Who would be half possessed

By his own nakedness?

> Waking's my care--
> I'll make a broken music, or I'll die
>   (CP 240).

Whereas in "In a Dark Time" the speaker rose to the dark freedom of the Godhead, he has now descended into the slowly falling dark of evening air: "A dark theme keeps me here" (CP 240). He is being held back by the darkness that comes to those who know the transient nature of the mystic consciousness. This is the darkness of the world that presses in upon one who suddenly lacks an intuition of the presence of the eternal in the temporal. He must awaken, even if at first he can only "make a broken music." The sense of having transcended time is now only a memory:

> Once I transcended time:
> A bud broke to a rose,
> And I rose from a last diminishing (CP 240).

As a bud broke its boundaries and opened wide to become a rose, so he once rose from death to life. "Waking's my care," he says. Once again he must begin the slow, dark process of simplifying the self to attain the unity of being symbolized by the rose. To aid him in his journey he calls upon "the small": "Ye littles, lie more close!" (CP 240).

In discussing purification of the self, Underhill identifies the contemplative with the prisoners in Plato's cave: "A literal and deliberate getting out of the cave must be for every mystic, as it was for Plato's prisoners, the first step in the individual hunt for reality" (M 199). Roethke's "hunt" began with a direct assault, but now that the speaker has plunged into the dark evening air he has returned to the cave. Surrounded by the shadows of evening, he has become lethargic. Looking down "a far light,"

Roethke's speaker beholds "the dark side of a tree,"
but when he looks again the vision has been "lost upon
the night" (CP 240). By embracing "Night . . . a dear
proximity," he attempts to hold on to the image that
the darkness has engulfed. But the things of this life
are illusory. The tree and the speaker will both feel
the effect of time in their growing and dying. In the
final stanza he stands near "a low fire / Counting the
wisps of flame" and watching the light shift "upon the
wall" (CP 240). Once again he attempts to control the
darkness, this time by bidding "stillness be still"
(CP 240). Seeing the shadows cast "in evening air,"
the speaker perceives "How slowly dark comes down on
what we do" (CP 240). Whether we write a poem or
endeavor to turn the self toward God, the way is slow
and dark.

"The Sequel" is a colloquy with the self in which
Roethke's speaker begins the work of the understanding
by descending into a purgative state of self-
analysis. "Was I too glib about eternal things?" he
asks (CP 241). He acknowledges that he has pursued
"Pure aimlessness" and the "wild longings of the
insatiate blood" until he has become a "weak moth
blundering by" (CP 241). Falling to his knees, he
recognizes that he cannot be "Both moth and flame," for
the self is being consumed. "Whom do we love?" he
asks. "I thought I knew the truth; / Of grief I died,
but no one knew my death" (CP 241). The "truth" that
he "thought" he knew in his glibness has receded into
the darkness. Now he doubts the validity of his
mystical experiences, for when he died of grief no one
seemed to notice. He has approached the contemplative
life in a superficial manner, becoming "An intimate of
air and all its song" (CP 241).

Memory and imagination come to the speaker's aid in the next two stanzas as he recalls a moment when he danced in the wind and transcended time. His partner is the anima, "A shape called up out of my natural mind" (CP 241). The anima, as Bremond has noted, is "the deep self" representing "mystical or poetic knowledge."[29] Bremond's animus/anima distinction between the surface and deep self is obviously based upon Jung's theories. Appropriately, then, Ralph Mills has interpreted Roethke's figure as "the anima or soul, which is a female principle in the male."[30] Roethke's vision of the two figures dancing "on and on" under "a dancing moon" is the first of several celebrations in the Sequence representing the union of body and soul. Their dance proclaims the spiritual awakening that the speaker has lost, a time when the two selves became one. In this mystical moment he "heard a bird stir in its true confine," the spirit waking in the core of the soul (CP 241). All of nature seems to respond to the stirring, participating in the dance. Even with "the coming of the outrageous dawn" the speaker believes that they "danced on and on" into eternity, for he has transcended time, and "Morning's" but "a motion in a happy mind" (CP 241). "As leaves live in the wind," so the anima breathes in light and air, "Swaying . . . like some long water weed" (CP 241). But soon she leaves him, a leaf swaying out on the wind:

> She left my body, lighter than a seed;
> I gave her body full and grave farewell.
> A wind came close, like a shy animal.
> A light leaf on a tree, she swayed away
> To the dark beginnings of another day
>   (CP 241).

The speaker becomes the tree, losing the anima "To the
dark beginnings of another day."

In the final stanza, with the dance ended, the
mind returns to its probing questions: "Was nature
kind? The heart's core tractable?" (CP 242). No
answers are given, but a clue is found in the
notebooks. Roethke's statement, "I found the heart's
core to be an almost intractable material," is a motif
in the notebooks, beginning as early as 1946 (6 #86).
As the heart is intractable, so nature is not always
"Kind," for "waters waver" and "fires fail," reminding
the speaker of his mortality. He begs the "leaves" to
"lean forth" and tell him what he is. As if in
response, a "single tree turns into purest flame,"
suggesting the processes of life as the seasons change
and all things move toward death. But this "slow fire"
is "denied" the speaker, for he has "denied desire,"
both physical and spiritual. He has become "a man at
intervals / Pacing a room, a room with dead-white
walls" (CP 242). Although he has imprisoned himself in
the "dead-white walls" of Plato's cave, he still feels
"the autumn fail" (CP 242). And he feels it more
intensely because he has denied the life-giving motion
that would cause him to turn into "purest flame." In
her "Fourth Meditation," the old woman prays for "the
self-involved": "How I wish them awake!" she says.
"May they flame into being!" (CP 169). Like the tree,
the speaker must become a blaze of being. He takes the
first step toward that end in the next poem.

Roethke's protagonist begins his long journey out
of the cave in "The Motion." The poem is a hymn to the
motions of love, both physical and spiritual, that
create the self's sense of stability. In terms of the
structure of the meditative sequence, "The Motion"

constitutes a discourse in which the protagonist comes
to a new understanding about the nature of the soul by
considering the "stretchings of the spirit" (CP 243).
Meditating on the meaning of motion, he learns that he
still has a chance "to be."

In "The Motion" Roethke's speaker analyzes the
motions of the soul, assuming for a moment the poise of
lover and mystic. Underhill believes that their
outlooks are the same, "for the mystic and lover, upon
different planes, are alike responding to the call of
the Spirit of Life" (M 89):

> Who but the loved know love's a faring-forth?
> Who's old enough to live?--a thing of earth
> Knowing how all things alter in the seed
> Until they reach this final certitude,
> This reach beyond this death, the act of love
> In which all creatures share, and thereby
>   live (CP 243).

"Love's a faring-forth," the speaker says, an activity
in which the self reaches out, stretching beyond its
boundaries. As "Mystic Love" is characterized by "the
deep-seated desire and tendency of the soul towards its
Source," so the lover seeks the loved one (M 46). This
"act of love," the sexual act and the soul's response
to God, "In which all creatures share, and thereby
live," is the one constancy amid the altering of all
things. Reaching "beyond this death," it creates the
"final certitude." The "faring-forth," the motion of
love itself, keeps us steady. As "Lust" keeps "the
mind alive," bringing "the certainty of love," so the
"stretchings of the spirit" extend the soul until it is
sustained by the knowledge of God's love.

"I dare embrace," the speaker says. "By striding,
I remain" (CP 243). The meaning of the paradox is

found not only in the act of love but also in the
stabilizing force of motion itself. "Motion is
meaning," Roethke comments in a 1952-53 notebook; "I
outfly eternity, for things in motion keep my being
still" (10 #138). If "the essence of spirit is
activity," then motion is a means by which the self
attains spiritual grace, the stillness of "final
certitude" (11 #150). In the poem, Roethke's emphasis
is on "striding," moving with the motion of life
itself. The speaker watches "An old wind-tattered
butterfly" pulsing "its wings upon the dusty ground" in
"stretchings of the spirit," and, like a child, his
hope is renewed:

O who would take the vision from the child?--
O, motion O, our chance is still to be!
                    (CP 243).

Stillness and motion are embraced as the speaker sees
that there is still a chance for him to attain true
being. "By striding, we remain."

Despite the vision of the "act of love" that
"reaches beyond this death," and in which "all
creatures share," the speaker is still possessed by
self-love, one aspect of his "Infirmity." Like
Narcissus, he "plays the constant fool" and stares in
the pool, telling himself "my image cannot die"
(CP 244). Loving the self and yet desiring the life of
the spirit, he exclaims, "Oh, to be something else, yet
still to be!" (CP 244). This is the cry of one who
longs for the mystic consciousness, but is afraid of
losing his identity in the moment of union with God.
In a tone of self-mockery he calls upon "Sweet Christ"
who has known the anguish of physical pain and
suffering to "rejoice in [his] infirmity": "There's
little left I care to call my own" (CP 244). When

fluid is drained from the knee and the shoulder is
pumped with cortisone, the speaker "conforms to [his]
divinity / . . . dying inward, like an aging tree"
(CP 244). But as the body begins to "break down," he
becomes conscious of "a pure extreme of light" suddenly
breaking in upon the mind. "The soul delights in that
extremity," the speaker says (CP 244). This blinding
radiance piercing the mind and soul suggests a movement
to a higher level of consciousness, that breakthrough
which characterizes the awakening of the self. It is
the "waking"--the "broken music"--that the speaker
longed for in the darkness of "In Evening Air"
(CP 240). Awakening, as Underhill has noted, is "an
intense form of the phenomenon of 'conversion,'" an
"'unselfing'" that occurs hand in hand with purification and gradually shades into the illuminated state
(M 176-77). These seemingly separate stages of the
mystic way merge in the following stanza as the speaker
becomes the "son and father," sufferer and creator, "of
[his] own death" (CP 244). Persisting in tones of
self-mockery and irony, he says "Blessed the meek; they
shall inherit wrath" (CP 244). Roethke's protagonist,
who is certainly not one of the meek, begins to accept
the on-coming of grace in the next stanza.

The activity of the mind begins to slow in stanza
three, producing an Interior Quiet in which the inner
eye, the eye of the soul, sees:

The deep eye sees the shimmer on the stone;
The eternal seeks, and finds, the temporal
(CP 244).

The transcendental self rises into full consciousness,
permitting the speaker to see in the dance of light
upon the stone that the Eternal still seeks and finds
man. The gradual change of the "slow moon" from "dark

to light" signals the speaker's conversion and self-
annihilation:

> Dead to myself, and all I hold most dear,
> I move beyond the reach of wind and fire
>   (CP 244).

As the mind deepens into contemplation, he seems to
transcend time and hears his dead selves singing "Deep
in the greens of summer" (CP 244). This "great day" of
revelation "balances upon the leaves" and this
"balance" creates the speaker's sense of equilibrium
and calm. Even when "all is still" he hears the song
of the vireo proclaiming the knowledge he has gained:
"My soul is still my soul, and still the Son"
(CP 244). His soul remains his own because it has not
been absorbed in God. The Son is "still," suggesting
that the active birth of Christ in the soul has not
occurred. Nevertheless, the speaker seems to have
touched the stillness of Christ in the midst of his
infirmity and states that he is "not yet undone"
(CP 244). He is ready to journey the difficult way
toward Eternity. "Things without hands take hands," he
says: "There is no choice,-- / Eternity's not easily
come by" (CP 244). During the journey he teaches
himself to perceive his mortality with the eyes and
ears of one who has attained the illuminated vision:

> When opposites come suddenly in place,
> I teach my eyes to hear, my ears to see
> How body from spirit does unwind
> Until we are pure spirit at the end
>   (CP 244).

Knowledge of the unwinding of the body comes when
opposites "balance" and the "pure extreme of light"
penetrates the soul, purifying the spirit.

Considering the poem as one stage in the
meditative process, we can see that "Infirmity" is an
analytical discourse in which the self ponders its
mortality with the aid of the understanding. The poem
moves from self-love and fear of death to a recognition
that "at the end" the decaying body becomes "pure
spirit." This is one of the central "points" of
Roethke's meditation, in the Ignatian sense, for in
"Infirmity" the speaker attains Quiet, experiencing
awakening, conversion, purification, and illumination. The knowledge that spiritual grace is still
possible prepares for "The Decision," a colloquy in
which the will finally acts.

"The Decision" marks the point in the middle of
the Sequence where the self begins to climb out of its
fear and turn toward God, "the invisible" that "shakes
the eye" (CP 245). "Running from God's the longest
race of all," the speaker says. This recognition and
the "turning" it produces are precipitated by the
memory of the phoebe's song that has haunted him since
he "was young." That sound--"The phoebe's slow
retreating from its song"--reminds him, even now, of
his lost childhood, "The sleepy sound of leaves in a
light wind" (CP 245). But it also symbolizes the
stirring of the spirit, the movement toward
"decision." This striving is heralded at the beginning
of the second stanza by two exclamations. "Rising or
falling's all one discipline!" proclaims the speaker
(CP 245). The way up and the way down are one
motion: one falls before he rises, dies in order to
live. This journey, as every contemplative knows,
imposes upon the self the darkness and pain of
purgation and requires obedience and instruction.
Suddenly he comes to a second realization: "The line

of my horizon's growing thin!" (CP 245). Like the old
woman, this speaker fears that his perpetual beginnings
have thinned the soul, the boundary line between time
and eternity. "Which is the way?" he cries to the
darkness and "the cinders at [his] back," the path
burned by his "running." Again he cries out like the
lost son, but no answer comes and no guide appears. He
"turns to go," facing the dark way with the courage and
determination of one who "turns to face oncoming snow"
(CP 245).

"The Marrow" depicts the protagonist's "long and
terrible way" from "me to Thee," an arduous spiritual
journey involving pain and spiritual death (CP 246).
It is a colloquy with the self and God in which
Roethke's speaker slays his will, yearning to "be near"
(CP 246). Moreover, "The Marrow" is one of the few
poems in which Roethke presents the forms of the Dark
Night of the Soul described in mystical literature.
The poem opens with despair and boredom, that
"spiritual ennui" which the ascetics call "'aridity'"
(M 391). The wind comes in from the sea, but it "says
nothing new," indicating the speaker's spiritual
lassitude. Instead of the vireo's song he hears "small
flies" singing in the "mist above [him]" and "the sharp
speech of a crow" telling him of his sin, that his
"drinking breeds a will to die" (CP 246). His only
thoughts are of the "worst portion of this mortal
life"--"A pensive mistress, and a yelping wife"
(CP 246).

Following his "decision," the speaker has been
beset by spiritual and emotional fatigue, but in stanza
two he begins "Brooding on God," thinking he "may
become a man" and thus achieve spiritual identity. He
contemplates God as the source of light, a light that

"dazzles all I see," a light so brilliant that "One
look too close can take my soul away" (CP 246).   Such
contemplation brings the "pain" of "a lost fire,"
burning with "Desire, desire, desire" (CP 246).   Love
and pain are united in the "dark ecstasy or 'pain of
God,'" an "invasion of a wild and unendurable desire to
'see God'" (M 394).   The intensity of his desire makes
him even more conscious of God's absence, causing him
to fear that the Godhead no longer exists.   In the
third stanza, then, Roethke's speaker cries out in
agony, "Godhead above my God, are you there still?"
(CP 246).   His plea is a colloquy or conversation in
which he acknowledges his death-in-life existence.
"The soul / That once could melt the dark with its
small breath" has been altered, he says, by his
decaying body (CP 246).   Believing that God is
abandoning him, he shouts the prayer, "Lord, hear me
out, and hear me out this day: / From me to Thee's a
long and terrible way" (CP 246).

The final stanza suggests how far he has journeyed
in his spiritual quest to "know."   "I was flung back
from suffering and love," he says, "When light divided
on a storm-tossed tree" (CP 246).   When the "pure
extreme of light" broke in upon him, delighting the
soul, he was thrown back from his "infirmity," his
self-love and physical suffering.   The "aging tree" of
the "Infirmity" that died "inward" is also the "storm-
tossed tree" pierced by light.   During this storm of
the spirit he has shifted between doubt and the
"dazzling dark" of mystical illumination (CP 155).   Now
that he has made the decision to stop running from God,
he has "slain [his] will," including the "will to die"
of stanza one, and his burning desire is to "be near"
(CP 246).   The striking light has shattered his will

and "still I live," he says, indicating that he has not
yet surrendered the self to God. Implied in his words
is the underlying fear that union will cause the death
of the self through absorption in God.

The person who realizes the Unitive Life speaks of
this union either as "deification," which is "the utter
transmutation of the Self in God" or as the "Spiritual
Marriage of his soul with God" [her italics] (M 415).
Underhill emphasizes that by deification the great
mystics do not mean that the self is identified with
God but rather that "a transfusion of their selves by
His Self" takes place (M 420). In other words, the
personality of the mystic is not absorbed in God but is
made more real. Similarly, Spiritual Marriage does not
mean "self-loss in an Essence, but self-fulfillment in
the union of heart and will" (M 426). The self is
transformed by abandoning the "I" to the direction of
the Will of God, thus realizing its true self.
Nevertheless, to one who has not experienced union, the
process will appear to be a loss of the "I" through
absorption.

Roethke's speaker purifies the will, but he does
not undergo the annihilation of selfhood by which the
self ceases to be "its 'own centre and circumference'"
(M 397). Such mortification requires breaking up "his
egoistic attachments and cravings, in order that the
higher centre, the 'new man,' may live and breathe"
(M 217). Instead of bringing to birth this spiritual
man, Roethke's protagonist "bleeds [his] bones,"
"bestowing their marrow" upon God as an atonement, a
gift bestowed "Upon that God who knows that I would
know" (CP 246). Bestowing one's marrow upon God is a
death peculiar to the Dark Night of the Soul, that dark
ecstasy which prepares for the final union whereby God

is received into what Ruysbroeck calls the "'marrow of
the Soul'" (M 68). Before this union can be
experienced, however, "The spark of the soul, the fast-
growing germ of divine humanity, must so invade every
corner of character that the self can only say with St.
Catherine of Genoa, "My me is God: nor do I know my
selfhood except in God'" (M 396) Roethke's protagonist
may not be able to climb out of his fear to surrender
his selfhood to God. At this stage in his journey he
must wait to experience a sense of God's presence.
Following his dark night, the speaker "waits" for "the
wind to move the dust," but at first no wind comes
(CP 247). Regeneration is what he desires in "I
waited": to be filled, as Underhill says, with "an
energy, a quickening Spirit, which comes from the soul,
and 'secretly initiates what He openly crowns'"
(M 122). Throughout Roethke's poetry, wind represents
the Holy Spirit, the breath of God the Creator that
animates all things. The speaker is waitng, then, for
the spark of life to be rekindled in his soul, the
divine spirit of desire that will make him conscious of
God's presence and love.

"I Waited" is a colloquy which separates the main
points of the meditation from the final acts of the
will. It depicts a state of waiting which represents
the receptivity of the self, a moment at once memory
and reality. At first the speaker is engulfed by air
so thick that he seems to eat it. The "level noise" of
the "meadow insects" is the only sound he hears, a
leveling that signals his rising. "I rose, a heavy
bulk, above the field," the speaker says (CP 247).
Despite his sensation of heaviness, of walking "in hay,
/ Deep in the mow, and each step deeper down," he seems
to be weightless, as if he "floated on the surface of a

pond" (CP 247). This paradoxical condition symbolizes
the mystical moment in which the speaker is lifted
"above the field" to glimpse nature in all its
"shimmering," the "dazzle" of its eternal idea. Once
again the field is the place of discovery where
Roethke's protagonist learns of the Eternals. This is
"the pure moment" at "the edge of the field" for which
the old woman waited in her "Fourth Meditation"
(CP 168), one of those times "when reality comes
closer: / In a field, in the actual air" (CP 166):

> I saw all things through water, magnified,
> And shimmering. The sun burned through a
>   haze,
> And I became all that I looked upon.
> I dazzled in the dazzle of a stone
>   (CP 247).

These lines clearly depict certain aspects of the
"lowest stage" of the "vision of unity" as described by
Rudolf Otto in Mysticism East and West. a work known by
Roethke. Otto's analysis indicates that the "Mysticism
of unifying vision" develops in three states: (1) a
perception of the unity of all created things; i.e.,
the one and the many in an organic whole; (2) a
perception of this unity as "One"; i.e., the many is
seen in the One and the One is seen in the many; and
(3) a perception of the Absolute One as a transcendent
reality in contrast to the many.[31] The first phase of
this vision is merely a preparation for the higher
stages and "is not in itself necessarily an attitude of
the mystical soul."[32] Its characteristics include the
identification of all created things; the vision of all
things in an eternal "Now" above time and space; the
transfiguration of all things to reveal their "eternal

idea"; the identification of the perceiver and the perceived.[33]

Roethke's poem illustrates the "transfiguration" of all things to reveal their "eternal idea" and the identification of the perceiver and the perceived. Nature has become transparent and luminous, filled with the light of God reflected by the water of the pond. Roethke quotes Eckhart in the notebooks: "Whoever forsakes things as they are accidental [sic] possesses them in as much as they are pure Being and Eternal-- Eckhart" (12 #176). A similar statement is found in Otto. Eckhart concludes with this image: "It is as when a man pours water into a clean vessel and lets it stand and then, if he holds his face over it he sees his face at the bottom (resplendent) as it is in itself."[34] Roethke's speaker sees nature "as it is in itself." So "dazzled" is he by "the dazzle of a stone," the presence of the Eternal burning through the "haze," that he sees "all things 'in himself,'" or, more precisely, 'as himself'--as not differentiated from himself."[35] He absorbs the intense light of the stone, becoming dazzled or blinded with wonder. This identification prepares for the sense of oneness at the end of the Sequence, the cosmic dance in which the speaker's true self participates.

The speaker's rising is brief; soon a jackass brays, a lizard leaps his foot, and he falls back down to "the dusty road." He turns to go, afraid to look back, walking as if his feet are "deep in sand." "I moved like some heat-weary animal," he says (CP 247). The way becomes "steeper," leading him "between stony walls." Finally he descends "through a rocky gorge" into a plateau overlooking a "bright sea" with its "level waves." Once again leveling signals a change:

"And all the winds came toward me. I was glad" (CP 247). When the Spirit of Love reaches out to him the speaker is filled with joy, a joy that becomes the ground of his being and the root of the final four poems of the Sequence.

"The Tree, The Bird" embodies the first of the spiritual acts with which Roethke concludes the meditative sequence. In his discussion of the meditative discipline, St. Francis de Sales noted that "Meditation moves our will to make spiritual acts" such as the "desire for heaven and eternal glory," and it "awakens a sense of compassion, wonder and joy."[36] This poem is one of the poet's most explicit representations of a mystical experience that employs images from the natural world, a moment of joy symbolizng the soul's stretch toward eternity. Once again the symbols of tree and bird appear, suggesting the body and the Spirit. Ultimately, the poem may be viewed as a dramatization of a statement which Roethke quotes in the notebooks, in this instance without naming the author: "'Eternity is the experience of holding and possessing in one moment the here and now, the past and present and that which is to come'" (14 #192). In the first two stanzas the speaker remembers an experience which is both in and outside this life, a timeless moment, while in the third stanza "the present falls away," revealing the pure "motion of the rising day," Eternity itself (CP 248).

The poem begins with the speaker's memory of walking through "stony fields" at midnight. He is "At ease with joy, a self-enchanted man" (CP 248). This self-enchantment is caused by the speaker's heightened consciousness of created nature during meditation: fields rise up to meet him, snails nod to him, light

meets him, and a voice calls to him from a cloud.
Their movement toward him indicates the extent to which
the self has penetrated the natural world, establishing
a relationship between the perceiver and the
perceived.[37]   But suddenly a change occurs.   When he
sighs, he stands outside this life:

> Yet when I sighed, I stood outside my life,
> A leaf unaltered by the midnight scene,
> Part of a tree still dark, still, deathly
>   still,
> Rising the air, a willow with its kind,
> Bearing its life and more, a double sound,
> Kin to the wind, and the bleak whistling rain
>   (CP 248).

This ecstasy (ek-stasis) or "standing-out" from himself
represents the beginning of his movement from the
material to the spiritual world.   He becomes a leaf,
part of a willow tree "still dark."   The deathly
stillness of the tree is terrifying, especially since
it carries with it the unbearable song of a bird that
grows louder, "altering / With every shift of air"
(CP 248).   Thus the willow bears "a double sound," its
own weeping in wind and rain and the song of the bird
with its "beating wings," symbolic of the Dove, the
Holy Spirit.   As if in answer to its call, the
speaker's soul responds with a "lonely buzz behind
[his] midnight eyes" (CP 248).   This "still cry" from
the ground or core of his soul, reminiscent of the
"heat-maddened summer fly" of "In a Dark Time," is the
buzz of the soul attempting to break through the
barrier of the body.   Its release comes during
contemplation as "the present falls away" to the pure
"motion of the rising day" and "The white sea widening
on a farther shore":

> The bird, the beating bird, extending
>   wings--.
> Thus I endure this last pure stretch of joy,
> The dire dimension of a final thing
>   (CP 248).

The motion and joy of this new day prepares for the
flight of the bird. Like the bird, Roethke's speaker
undergoes the pressure and strain of the beating,
extending wings as his soul takes flight toward the
Eternal. He "endures" a "stretch of joy," a pulling or
widening as if he is being extended across space and
lifted up to Eternity.[38] This widening is clearly the
result of the speaker's deepening contemplation. The
joy of the soul reaching out toward him stretches the
speaker, causing a strain that must be "endured." Such
joy is "The dire dimension of a final thing," for there
is an element of dread in the extremity of the spirit
that takes the speaker beyond the self, thus
threatening its existence. Despite its fear, the self
has responded to the deep "mother-root" of the soul's
"still cry" (CP 248). The speaker's experience of
"this last pure stretch of joy" during contemplation
anticipates the unity of being depicted in "The
Restored."

Roethke's conviction that the intuitive vision
surpasses rational thought as a means of apprehending
Reality is dramatized in "The Restored" in the form of
a narrated colloquy between the self and the soul.
This way of un-knowing must be regained if the self is
to experience the cosmic dance at the end of the
Sequence. The soul drops "as if shot," "maimed" by
"thought"; but when "reason" fails and the self rages
and wails, the soul grows another wing and dances.
Roethke makes clever use of dialogue and rhyme, but his

point is quite clear: intuition and emotion are the
life of the soul.   St. Bernard calls the mystic
consciousness "'the soul's true unerring intuition, the
unhesitating apprehension of truth'" (M 50).   Once the
intellect or "conscious mind" is passive, Underhill
says, "the more divine mind below the threshold--organ
of our free creative life--can emerge and present its
reports" (M 64).   This "sense" or faculty known as the
mystic or poetic consciousness has the power of
perceiving the "supersensual--the intelligible world
[her italics]" (M 50).   Thus when reason fails and the
mind slows in contemplation, the soul regains its
ability to fly up above the temporal and see into
eternity.   In "The Restored" this vision is
communicated through the soul's dance, a joyous
celebration of wholeness of being:

> And danced, at high noon,
> On a hot, dusty stone,
> In the still point of light
> Of my last midnight (CP 249).

Roethke's image of the soul dancing "In the still point
of light" expresses the reconciliation between movement
and stillness.   At this moment, Eternity is known in
the extremity of the soul and the speaker experiences
his "last midnight."   His dark broodings are dispelled
in the joy of the dance.   As the soul pivots, balancing
in the light of the "still point," Roethke's speaker
embraces and gathers to himself the contraries at the
heart of Pure Being.   A similar experience is recorded
in the notebooks: "My eyes brood on a point of light
so fine / I spin out into space, pure on the wind" (14
#200).   The speaker's use of Ordinary Contemplation has
produced an Illuminated Vision, a revelation of the
mystery at the heart of Being.   His soul restored,

Roethke's speaker celebrates his "last midnight." Now he becomes "the happy man," a man to whom "The Right Thing" happens.

"The Right Thing" is an intricate villanelle that examines the nature of the spiritual man the speaker has become. Although it is not written in the first person, the poem is nevertheless one of the speaker's final acts of praise and thanksgiving. Roethke describes "the happy man" as a man who no longer "probes" and "delves" the mystery of the motion of life. He leaves that to the "Time-harried prisoners of Shall and Will," men who think they "can" impose their will on an every-changing reality, men who think they are capable of fathoming the mystery (CP 250). Those who are unwilling to renounce their wills are trapped by time and will never live on those higher levels where the self may be merged with the great life of the All. As Eckhart says, "'He alone has spiritual poverty who wills nothing, knows nothing, desires nothing'" (6 #88). Thus the "happy man" is the one who recognizes that reason cannot probe the mystery. Instead, Roethke's speaker "Takes to himself what mystery he can," "surrendering his will" to the Infinite Will "Till mystery is no more: No more he can" (CP 250). Clearly, the words "will" and "can" are the most important words in the poem. Roethke emphasizes the word "can" by varying the first refrain line of the villanelle.

Richard Blessing has already discussed the changes Roethke has made in the villanelle form, but this aspect requires further comment.[39] The opening refrain, "Let others probe the mystery if they can," should be repeated at the ends of tercets two and four and again in the quatrain. Instead, Roethke alters the

line each time it appears. Through this incremental
repetition, Roethke communicates the essence of the
poem's meaning. Like the self, this line undergoes a
transmutation. In its final form it reads, "Till
mystery is no more: No more he can" (CP 250). Thus
the line develops until we see that "the happy man" is
the one who submits his will to the Will of the All and
admits, "No more he can." No more does he possess the
ability, power or right to control or shape his
destiny, or to delve into the mystery of why "The hill
becomes the valley, and is still" (CP 250). No more is
he concerned with the small becoming great, the great
becoming small, for he is no longer a prisoner of
"Shall and Will." He has learned to float on the
surface of the pond, moving with the current, and thus
he praises "change as the slow night comes on"
(CP 250). By accepting change as a natural element in
the process of things, he can embrace the mystery.

After slaying his will and bestowing his bone
marrow upon God, Roethke's protagonist has become "the
happy man," a "Child of the dark" who is both moving
and still. This paradox is emphasized by the contrast
between the evolving first line and the constant
refrain, "The right thing happens to the happy man"
(CP 250). He has attained the centrality of being that
permits him to "out leap the sun" or to sit still, "a
solid figure when / The self-destructive shake the
common wall" (CP 250). The happy man possesses the
stability that allows the spirit to soar, a rootedness
that stems from his unity of being: "God bless the
roots!--Body and soul are one!" Roethke's protagonist
has moved from multiplicity to unity, from the self
toward the All. Now that "His being" is "single"
(whole), he is ready to acknowledge his participation

in "that being" that is "all," a participation that
will create the eternal dance of the soul (CP 250).

"Once More, The Round" embodies the ultimate
spiritual act of Roethke's meditation, a joyful dance
of affirmation and praise. The poem's opening
question--"What's greater, Pebble or Pond?"--indicates
the concern of the self as it draws toward the
Eternal. But the protagonist's fear has been
dispelled, for he has learned to float on the surface
of the pond, moving in accordance with the motion of
life. The one who ran from God discovers that the
"Unknown" can be known. He has let go of metaphysical
speculation and recovered the intuitive vision--
thinking by feeling, not knowing. Purged of the
phenomenal self in "Infirmity" and the will in "The
Marrow," the protagonist becomes the "true self"
running toward "a Hill" to see "More! O More!"
(CP 251). Now that the "true self" has been realized,
there is no longer the question of "Which I is I?" for
body and soul are one. Lifted up by the transcendental
self, he comes to a new vision, perceiving with "the
Eye altering all" (CP 251). As Blake says, "'The tree
which moves some to tears of joy is in the eyes of
others only a green thing which stands in the
way. . . . As a man is, so he sees. As the eye is
formed, such are its powers'" (M 259). Roethke's
protagonist has moved to a higher consciousness that
permits "the Eye" to apprehend the "otherness" and the
hidden unity of all things. This new vision causes him
to "dance with William Blake," his visionary guide,
"for Love's sake" (CP 251).

Like the musical form, Roethke's "round" is a
continuous, circular dance, symbolizing the speaker's
experience of unity. It creates a polyphonic texture

of Bird, Leaf, Fish and Snail participating in the cosmic dance. These elements of nature are part of the "life" that he has come to "adore." As Roethke says in the notebooks, "I have entered into an alliance with all creatures" (15 #221). Clearly, the way up has been the way down; for the speaker has "descended," finally, "into a more human, a more realizable condition," arriving at a "shared love," a dance in which "abiding Leaf" and "the questing Snail" participate (13 #192). Roethke's speaker affirms the unity of the created world:

> And everything comes to One,
> As we dance on, dance on, dance on
> (CP 251).

Through this dance that goes on and on into Eternity, Roethke unifies all the seeming dichotomies in his poetry. "Everything comes to One": the one and the many, the self and the other, the temporal and the eternal. In a 1958 notebook entry Roethke records these quotations by Eckhart and Plotinus from Otto's analysis of "the lowest stage" of the "vision of unity":

lowest stage

> "In the eternal goodness of the divine nature (as in a miraculous mirror) the essence of all creatures is seen as one."
> "Therefore All is everywhere"
> Plotinus (12 #176)[40]

Roethke's speaker goes beyond this initial stage wherein the one and the many are perceived in an organic whole, for this unity is brought to One. Of this second stage Otto says: "'The One' is no longer a predicate of the many but becomes an equation of the One and the many: Many is one, and the One is

many."[41]   In the midst of this equation, the One comes
to the fore and is seen in the many. Fundamentally,
Roethke's vision of unity is a panenhenic experience
which he defines in "On 'Identity'": "the sense that
all is one and one is all" (SP 26). However, his
perception of "everything coming to One" also
represents the attainment of the second stage of Otto's
"vision of unity." Instead of losing his identity in
union with the All, a self-loss which should be a
transformation, Roethke's speaker sees the created
unity of all things and the One in the All. Roethke
quotes this statement from The Imitation of Christ in
the notebooks but without recording his source: "'He
to whom all things are one and who draweth all things
to one and seeth all things in one may be stable in
heart and peaceably abide in God'" (14 #203). By
drawing all things to One, the dance keeps him
steady.   Continuing to "draw near," Roethke's
protagonist dances on and on, participating in the
hidden harmony of the universe, the Eternal present in
the temporal.

     "Sequence, Sometimes Metaphysical" culminates in
motion, not stasis, a dance of praise in which the
"true self" participates. It is a dance that creates
its own stillness, for "Body and soul are one!" (CP
250). Roethke's protagonist has come to this condition
by an arduous meditative process involving despair,
waiting, self-annihilation, renunciation of the will,
acceptance of the soul's longing for Eternity, and
praise. As Meditation has deepened into Ordinary
Contemplation, he has experienced an Illuminated
Vision, partaking of the unity of Being. In those
moments of waiting when he has yielded his will to the
Supreme Will that moves the universe, he has been

touched by the Spirit of the creative source of life. Perpetual beginner, "child of the dark," the protagonist has learned by going where he had to go. The motion of the quest and the transmutation of the self have brought him finally to a sense of Divine unity. He has attained the selfhood which he sought so desperately, "A body with the motion of a soul" (CP 188).

CONCLUSION

```
Mystics:       outside to inside (mystic=one
               experience)

Poets:         inside to outside (multitude of
               experiences)
                    --Roethke Notebooks (6 #88)
```

Our wisdom increases, but does our
desire to convey it stay the same? I
think not. For there is something in
the psychology of the mystical precept
'he who knows does not speak.'
                    --Roethke Notebooks (6 #89)

These passages from Roethke's 1946 notebooks, though written early in his career, express his perception of the differences between the poetic and mystical experiences; an understanding that had become even more real to him by the end of this life, after practicing meditation and contemplation during the creative process. For the mystic, the experience of unitive contemplation with the Absolute is a single experience, one in which, as Meister Eckhart would say, God's Son is born in the soul. In Roethke's thinking, this is a movement from "outside to inside," a mystical action by which God is known in the deepest self, the Anima, and by which the will is affected. Through this union, the self names this Reality as God and responds with acts of charity by the grace of the Divine Will. For the poet, especially one who is a perpetual beginner, moving from anxiety and fear to freedom and joy, engaging in recurring colloquies with the self, the experience is from "inside to outside"; a series of long meditations by which he re-creates the self and progresses toward the creative order of the mind of God. The nature of these two experiences is clarified further by Raissa Maritain in The Situation of Poetry:

> Here, in the mystical experience, the
> object touched is the uncreated Abyss,
> God the savior and vivifier, known
> obscurely as present and united with the
> soul of him who contemplates; while the
> obscure knowledge which is that of the
> Poet, and which touches, as object
> known, the things and the reality of the
> word rather than God himself, flows from
> a union of another order, more or less
> intense, with God the creator and
> organizer of nature.[1]

While the poet touches God the creator, enjoying a
clarity of perception, a heightening of vision
concerning the phenomenal world, the mystic
participates in "conscious union with a living
Absolute," involving the "joyous loss of the
transfigured self in God" (M 73, 447). As Underhill
explains, "In mysticism the will is united with the
emotions in an impassioned desire to transcend the
sense-world, in order that the self may be joined by
love to the one eternal and ultimate Object of love" (M
71). The poet, as Roethke knew, is bound by words and
the sense-world.

The paths of the poet and the mystic are distinct
in another way, as Roethke implies in the second
notebook entry: one progresses toward the created
word, while the other moves toward the silence of
mystical contemplation. Both experiences are born near
the center of the soul, yet as Jacques Maritain states:

> Poetic experience is from the very start
> oriented toward expression, and
> terminates in a word uttered, or a work
> produced; while mystical experience

tends toward silence, and terminates in
an imminent fruition of the absolute.[2]
The poet employs meditation, withdrawing the faculties
in interior silence, and may even experience the
illuminated vision afforded by natural contemplation,
as does Roethke; but when he returns with the poetic
knowledge of the self and the revelation of the eternal
in the temporal, it is to write a poem. The mystic, on
the other hand, by the bond with God, will find that
his contemplative life is deepened and his acts of love
increased. As Meister Eckhart attests, "'What we have
gathered in contemplation, we give out in love'--
Eckhart" (15 #210). This 1962 notebook entry
underscores Roethke's awareness of the fruits of the
contemplative life, but the distinction between poet
and mystic remains: the poet communicates in images,
while the mystic rests in a contemplation that is
formless. Apparently Roethke's ultimate desire was to
find a path by which poet and mystic would become one,
as these passages from the 1950's suggest:

> To reject images in a formless
> contemplation of God (9 #185).
> Perhaps the true poet's path is closer
> to the mystic than we think: his
> thought becomes more imageless (13
> #185).

During contemplation the poet's thought may become
imageless, yet creativeness requires words and
images. Roethke may have yearned for that "formless
contemplation of God" which is the mark of the life of
the contemplative, but his withdrawal of the faculties
in meditation and contemplation culminated in words,
not silence.

The poetry created by Roethke embodies the
revelation which is the fruit of his practice of
meditation and natural contemplation. It is a unifying
vision grounded in his "sacramental view of nature"
(5 #65). Roethke comments in "On 'Identity'" that he
experienced a "feeling of the oneness of the universe,"
an intuition which is dramatized in the cosmic dance at
the end of "Sequence, Sometimes Metaphysical":

> . . . the 'oneness', is, of course, the
> first stage in mystical illumination, an
> experience many men have had, and still
> have: the sense that all is one and one
> is all. . . . This experience has come
> to me so many times, in so many varying
> circumstances, that I cannot suspect its
> validity: it is not one of the devil's
> traps, an hallucination, a voice, a
> snare (SP 26).

The foundation of Roethke's panenhenic experience of
oneness, and indeed of all the mystical moments in the
poetry, is best expressed in this statement by Robert
Sencourt which Roethke recorded in a 1962-63 notebook:

> 'Everything, if looked at rightly, is
> but a symbol and therefore a disclosure,
> of things unseen and of the underlying
> reality which is the mind of God'--
> Robert Sencourt (15 #216).

Roethke shares with William Blake and Jacob Boehme a
vision of the World of Becoming as infused by a spirit
that touches the invisible order of the universe. For
Roethke, "Everything that lives is holy" (SP 24). His
poetic world manifests the sacred and therefore points
beyond itself. Rooted in a belief in the sacredness of
all living things, Roethke's poetry demonstrates an

expansion of consciousness which entails, as Underhill
notes, "the discovery of the Perfect One self-revealed
in the Many, not the forsaking of the Many in order to
find the One" (M 254). This is the essential nature of
Roethke's vision of unity, a discovery peculiar to
poets, not mystics.

Roethke explained in "On 'Identity'" that his
vision of the oneness of all things was "inevitably
accompanied by a loss of the 'I,' the purely human ego,
to another center, a sense of the absurdity of death, a
return to a state of innocency" (SP 26). These are the
themes which characterize Roethke's approach to the
meditative genre.   They describe the strivings of
Roethke's protagonists to reach and embrace the deeper
self, to be released from the anxiety over non-being,
and to recover unity of being. Their struggle is to
know the true self and to become plain—a simple being
who intuits the presence of the eternal in the
temporal.   Through the use of ordinary or natural
contemplation they attain a new perception of reality,
the fruits of which are analyzed by Underhill in
Practical Mysticism: ". . . the emphasis upon the
message from without, rather than on their own reaction
to and rearrangement of it" and the exchange of the
self-centered, "false imagination" which distorts
sensations for the "true imagination" which follows its
intuitions and stretches out toward the greater
universe (PM 27).   Roethke's meditative sequences
dramatize not only the motions of the mind in search of
centrality of being but, more importantly, the
stretchings of the self to become a soul, to set its
bearings in the total universe.

NOTES

Chapter I

Introduction

[1] Jacques Maritain, <u>Creative Intuition in Art and Poetry</u> (Cleveland & New York: Meridian Books, The World Publishing Company, 1966), pp. 67, 82.

[2] Ibid., p. 83.

[3] Ibid., p. 85.

[4] Abbe Henri Bremond, <u>Prayer and Poetry</u>, trans. Algar Thorold (London: Burns, Oates, & Washbourne, 1927), pp. 108-09. Bremond's study is mentioned several times in Roethke's notebooks of the early 1950's.

[5] <u>On the Poet and His Craft: Selected Prose of Theodore Roethke</u>, ed. Ralph J. Mills, Fr. (Seattle: University of Washington Press, 1965), p. 25. Hereafter cited in the text as <u>SP</u>.

[6] Evelyn Underhill, <u>Mysticism: A Study in the Nature and Development of Man's Spiritual Consciousness</u> (12th ed. New York: Meridian Books, 1970), p. 67. This edition was included in Roethke's private library. The notebooks indicate that Roethke read Underhill in the early 1940's. Hereafter cited in the text as <u>M</u>.

[7] Maritain, <u>Creative Intuition in Art and Poetry</u>, pp. 78-79.

[8] Ibid., p. 70.

[9] Ibid., p. 71.

[10] Arnold Stein, "Introduction," <u>Theodore Roethke: Essays on the Poetry</u>, ed. Arnold Stein (Seattle: University of Washington Press, 1965), p. xiv.

[11] See Maritain, <u>Creative Intuition in Art and Poetry</u>, p. 191.

[12] Stein, "Introduction," <u>Theodore Roethke: Essays on the Poetry</u>, p. xiii.

[13] Evelyn Underhill, Practical Mysticism (New York: E. P. Dutton & Company, 1919), pp. 11, 26. Hereafter cited in the text as PM.

[14] Theodore Roethke, "On 'In a Dark Time,'" The Contemporary Poet as Artist and Critic, ed. Anthony Ostroff (Boston: Little, Brown and Company, 1964), p. 49.

[15] Theodore Roethke, The collected Poems of Theodore Roethke, (Garden City, New York: Doubleday and Company, 1966), p. 250.   Hereafter cited in the text as CP.

[16] Neal Bowers in Theodore Roethke: The Journey from I to Otherwise, (Columbia & London: University of Missouri Press, 1982) analyzes Roethke's collected poetry as developing according to three categories of mystical symbols, noting the existence of the five-step mystic way within each division and the poetry as a whole.   Bowers considers Roethke a mystical poet and, therefore, he discusses the poetry as mystical, not meditative.

[17] Neal Bowers, on pp. 79-80, does not distinguish between meditation and contemplation or delineate the three forms of contemplation.

[18] Louis L. Martz, The Poetry of Meditation, rev. ed. (New Haven: Yale University Press, 1962), p. 330.

[19] Ibid., p. 332.

[20] Meister Eckhart, ed. and trans. Raymond Bernard Blakney (New York: Harper and Brothers Publishers, 1941), p. 96.

[21] Martz, The Poetry of Meditation, p. 38.

[22] St. Francis de Sales, Introduction to the Devout Life, trans. Michael Day (London: Burns and Bates, 1956).   A copy of St. Francis' Introduction was included in Roethke's library.

[23] The Text of the Spiritual Exercises of Saint Ignatius, trans. John Morris (4th ed., Westminster, Maryland: Newman Bookshop, 1943).

[24] St. Francis de Sales, Introduction to the Devout Life, pp. 56-61.

^{25} The Text of the Spiritual Exercises of Saint
Ignatius, pp. 54-56.

Chapter II

The Lost Son Sequence

"A Field for Revelation

^{1} Maritain, Creative Intuition in Art and Poetry,
p. 91.

^{2} Ibid., pp. 92, 93.

^{3} Ibid., p. 93.

^{4} Ibid., p. 89.

^{5} The Text of the Spiritual Exercises of Saint
Ignatius, p. 54.

^{6} Ibid.

^{7} Ibid.

^{8} Mircea Eliade, Patterns in Comparative Religion,
(London: Sheed and Ward, 1958), p. 216.

^{9} Rudolf Otto, Mysticism East and West: A
Comparative Analysis of the Nature of Mysticism, trans.
Bertha L. Bracey and Richenda C. Payne (New York: The
Macmillan Company, 1932), pp. 45-46. A copy of Otto's
work was included in Roethke's private library.

^{10} William Wordsworth, The Prelude (1805), ed. E.
de Selincourt (London: Oxford University Press, 1960),
chap. I, lines 344-50.

^{11} St. Francis de Sales, Introduction to the
Devout Life, p. 58.

^{12} Henry Vaughan, The Complete Poetry of Henry
Vaughan, ed. French Fogle (New York: New York
University Press, 1965), p. 419.

^{13} Meister Eckhart, ed. and trans. Raymond Bernard
Blakney (New York: Harper and Brothers Publishers,
1941), p. 216.

¹⁴ William R. Inge, Christian Mysticism, (8th ed. London: Methuen and Company, Ltd., 1948), p. 31. This edition of Inge's study was included in Roethke's library.

Chapter III

"Meditations of an Old Woman"

Stretching Toward Humility

¹ Maritain, Creative Intuition in Art and Poetry, p. 177.

² Ibid., 179.

³ Ibid.

⁴ Ibid.

⁵ Ibid., pp. 179-80.

⁶ Ibid., p. 181.

⁷ The Text of the Spiritual Exercises of Saint Ignatius, p. 20. Cf. St. Francis de Sales' Introduction, pp. 56-57.

⁸ Theodore Roethke in On the Poet and His Craft: Selected Prose of Theodore Roethke, ed. Ralph J. Mills, Jr. (Seattle: University of Washington Press, 1965). p. 39.

⁹ See Karl Malkoff, Theodore Roethke: An Introduction to the Poetry (New York: Columbia University Press, 1966), p. 168; Richard Blessing, Theodore Roethke's Dynamic Vision (Bloomington: Indiana University Press, 1974), p. 137.

¹⁰ Meister Eckhart, pp. 167-68.

¹¹ Ibid., p. 163.

¹² Charles Bennett, a Philosophical Study of Mysticism (New Haven: Yale University Press, 1923), p. 101. Bennett's study is mentioned twice in Roethke's notebooks (12 #166; 15 #221). #17 in Article

[13] John Crowe Ransom, "On Theodore Roethke's 'In a Dark Time,'" The Contemporary Poet as Artist and Critic, ed. Anthony Ostroff (Boston: Little, Brown and Company, 1964), p. 32.

[14] Rosemary Sullivan, Theodore Roethke: The Garden Master (Seattle: University of Washington Press, 1975), p. 127.

[15] Nicolas Berdyaev, Freedom and the Spirit, trans. Oliver Fielding Clarke (4th ed. London: Geoffrey Bless: the Centenary Press, 1948), p. 62. This edition was included in Roethke's library.

Chapter IV

"North american Sequence"

Discovering the Hidden Self

[1] In a 1944 notebook entry Roethke speaks of writing "a long poem that would represent symbolically the condition of the American psyche, the American spiritual psyche. I seem to be increasingly concerned with the spiritual man, the American spiritual man" (5 #69).

[2] Meister Eckhart, p. 214.

[3] Paul Tillich, The Eternal Now (New York: Charles Scribner's Sons, 1963). pp. 125, 131.

[4] Rudolf Otto in The Idea of the Holy, trans. John W. Harvey (2nd ed. London: Oxford University Press, 1970). p. 6, invents the word "numinous" to "stand for 'the holy' minus its moral factor or 'moment,' and, . . . minus its 'rational' aspect altogether." This edition of Otto's work was included in Roethke's library.

[5] Berdyaev, Freedom and the Spirit, p. 241.

[6] The second edition of Martin Buber's I and Thou was included in Roethke's library and several quotations from the work appear in the notebooks of 1961-62.

[7] G. E. Bentley, Jr., "Introduction," William
Blake, Tiriel (Oxford: Clarendon Press, 1967),
pp. 6-7. Cf. Malkoff, Introduction to the Poetry,
p. 182.

[8] For other interpretations of this figure see
Blessing, Dynamic Vision, p. 153 and Sullivan, The
Garden Master, pp. 161-62.

[9] William Blake, The Marriage of Heaven and Hell,
Introd. and Commentary, Sir Geoffrey Keynes (London &
New York: Oxford University Press, 1975), p. xxii.

[10] Cf. Malkoff, Introduction to the Poetry,
p. 188.

[11] Cf. Jay Parini, Theodore Roethke: An American
Romantic (Amherst, Massachusetts: University of
Massachusetts Press, 1979), pp. 168-70 and Harry
Williams, 'The Edge Is What I Have': Theodore Roethke
and After (Lewisburg, Pennsylvania: Bucknell
University Press, 1977), pp. 117-18.

[12] One source of Roethke's understanding of the
pre-Socratics was Werner Jaeger's The Theology of the
Early Greek Philosophers (Oxford: The Clarendon Press,
1948). A copy of Jaeger's study is among Roethke's
annotated volumes in the Roethke Collection, Seattle.

[13] For discussion of these elements see Hugh
Staples, "Rose in the Sea-Wind: A Reading of Theodore
Roethke's 'North American Sequence,' " American
Literature, 36 (1964), 195; Sullivan, The Garden
Master, pp. 152-53; Blessing, Dynamic Vision,
pp. 138-56.

[14] Inge, Christian Mysticism, p. 5.

[15] William James, The Varieties of Religious
Experience, ed. Joseph Ratner (New Hyde Park, New
York: University Books, 1963), p. 388.

Chapter V

"Sequence, Sometimes Metaphysical"

Looking With a Hunter's Eye Toward Eternity

[1] Underhill, Practical Mysticism, p. 96.
Hereafter cited in the text as PM.

[2] Inge, Christian Mysticism, p. 10.

[3] Otto, The Idea of the Holy, p. 25. See also 9 #121 in The Roethke Notebooks.

[4] "The Abyss" does not follow Underhill's five-step mystic way as rigidly as William H. Heyen suggests in "The Divine Abyss: Theodore Roethke's Mysticism, "Texas Studies in Literature and Language, 11 (1969), 1051-1068.

[5] Jacob Boehme, Six Theosophic Points, trans. John Rolleston Earle, Introd., "Unground and Freedom," Nicholas Berdyaev (Ann Arbor: University of Michigan Press, 1970), p. XIV.

[6] Meister Eckhart, pp. 167-68.

[7] Heyen, p. 1061.

[8] Ibid., pp. 1059-61.

[9] Heyen, p. 1064.

[10] The Cloud of Unknowing, edited from the British Museum Manuscripts, Introd. Evelyn Underhill (4th ed. London: John M. Watkins, 1946). This edition of Cloud was included in Roethke's library.

[11] Bowers, The Journey from I to Otherwise, p. 172.

[12] Otto, The Idea of the Holy, p. 12.

[13] William Johnston, The Mysticism of the Cloud of Unknowing (New York: Desclee Company, 1967), p. 90.

[14] Ibid., p. 260.

[15] The Cloud of Unknowing, p. 189.

[16] The Soul Afire: Revelations of the Mystics, ed. H. R. Reinhold (New York: Pantheon Books, 1944), p. 19.

[17] Theodore Roethke, "On 'In a Dark Time,'" The Contemporary Poet as Artist and Critic, p. 49. Hereafter cited in the text as DT.

[18] Blessing, Dynamic Vision, p. 61.

[19] Thomas Aquinas, "Summa Theologica," Basic Writings of Saint Thomas Aquinas, ed. Anton C. Pegis (New York: Random House, 1945), I, 64.

[20] "When the spirit is ready, God enters it without hesitation or waiting," Meister Eckhart, p. 121.

[21] Vincent Buckley, Poetry and the Sacred (New York: Barnes and Noble, Inc., 1968), p. 50.

[22] Inge, Christian Mysticism, p. 121.

[23] Otto, The Idea of the Holy, trans, pref. John W. Harvey, p. xviii.

[24] "The Dark Night," The Collected Works of St. John of the Cross, trans. Kieran Kavanaugh and Otilio Rodriguez (Garden City, New York: Doubleday & Company, Inc., 1964), p. 338.

[25] Bowers, The Journey from I to Otherwise, p. 182.

[26] Boehme, Six Theosophic Points, Introd., "Unground and Freedom," Nicolas Berdyaev, pp. xx-xxiii.

[27] Meister Eckhart, pp. 200-01.

[28] Ibid., p. 98.

[29] Bremond, Prayer and Poetry, pp. 108-09.

[30] Ralph J. Mills, Jr., "In the Way of Becoming: Roethke's Last Poems," Theodore Roethke: Essays on the Poetry, ed. Arnold Stein (Seattle: University of Washington Press, 1965), p. 131.

[31] Otto, Mysticism East and West, pp. 44-52.

[32] Ibid., p. 54.

[33] Ibid., pp. 44-48.

[34] Ibid., p. 46.

[35] Ibid., p. 47.

[36] St. Francis de Sales, Introduction to the Devout Life, p. 58.

[37] Malkoff, Introduction to the Poetry, p. 217, interprets these lines, correctly I think, as the experience of "an 'I-Thou' relationship with every existing thing."

[38] See also Blessing's discussion of the pun on the word "stretch," Dynamic Vision, p. 215.

[39] Ibid., p. 217.

[40] Roethke does not cite Otto and he even omits Eckhart's name as the source of the first quotation, but the passage is clearly from Otto's Mysticism East and West, p. 44.

[41] Ibid., p. 49.

Conclusion

[1] Jacques and Raissa Maritain, The Situation of Poetry: Four Essays on the Relations Between Poetry, Mysticism, Magic, and Knowledge (New York: Philosophical Library, Inc., 1955), pp. 16-17.

[2] Maritain, Creative Intuition in Art and Poetry, p. 173.

SELECTED BIBLIOGRAPHY

SELECTED BIBLIOGRAPHY

Works by Theodore Roethke

The Collected Poems of Theodore Roethke. Garden City, New York: Doubleday and Company, Inc., 1966.

The Notebooks. Theodore Roethke Collection. University of Washington Library, Seattle.

"On 'In a Dark time.'" The Contemporary Poet as Artist and Critic. Ed. Anthony Ostroff. Boston: Little, Brown and Company, 1964.

On the Poet and His Craft: Selected Prose of Theodore Roethke. Ed. Ralph J. Mills, Jr. Seattle: University of Washington Press, 1965.

Selected Letters of Theodore Roethke. Ed. Ralph J. Mills, Jr. Seattle: University of Washington Press, 1968.

Straw for the Fire: From the Notebooks of Theodore Roethke 1943-63. Selected and arranged by David Wagoner. Garden City, New York: Doubleday and Company, Inc., 1972.

Works About Theodore Roethke

Arnett, Carroll. "Minimal to Maximal: Theodore Roethke's Dialectic." College English, 18 (1957), 414-16.

Blessing, Richard A. Theodore Roethke's Dynamic Vision. Bloomington: Indiana University Press, 1974.

Bowers, Neal. Theodore Roethke: The Journey from I to Otherwise. Columbia & London: University of Missouri Press, 1982.

Brown, Dennis E. "Theodore Roethke's 'Self-World' and the Modernist Position." Journal of Modern Literature, 3 (1974), 1239-54.

Burke, Kenneth. "The Vegetal Radicalism of Theodore Roethke." Sewanee Review, 58 (1950), 68-108.

Dickey, James. "Correspondences and Essences." Virginia Quarterly Review, 37 (1961), 635-40.

_____. "Theodore Roethke." Poetry, 105 (1964), 119-122.

Heyen, William. "The Divine Abyss: Theodore Roethke's Mysticism." Texas Studies in Literature and Language, 11 (1969), 1051-1068.

_____. Profile of Theodore Roethke. Columbus, Ohio: Charles E. Merrill Company, 1971.

_____. "Theodore Roethke's Minimals." Minnesota Review, 8 (1968), 359-375.

Kramer, Hilton. "The Poetry of Theodore Roethke." Western Review, 18 (1954), 131-154.

Kunitz, Stanley. "Roethke: Poet of Transformations." New Republic, 152 (January 23, 1965), 23-29.

La Belle, Jenijoy. The Echoing Wood of Theodore Roethke. Princeton, N.J.: Princeton University Press, 1976.

Libby, Anthony. "Roethke, Water Father." American Literature, 46 (1974), 267-288.

Malkoff, Karl. Theodore Roethke: An Introduction to the Poetry. New York: Columbia University Press, 1966.

Martz, William J. The Achievement of Theodore Roethke. Glenview, Illinois: Scott, Foresman and Company, 1966.

McClatchy, J. D. "Sweating Light from a Stone: Identifying Theodore Roethke." Modern Poetry Studies, 3 (1972), 1-24.

McMichael, James. "The Poetry of Theodore Roethke." The Southern Review, NS 5 (1969), 4-25.

Mills, Ralph J. Jr. "Keeping the Spirit Spare." Chicago Review, 13 (1959), 114-122.

_____. "Roethke's Last Poems." Poetry, 105 (1964), 122-124.

_____. Theodore Roethke. Minneapolis: University of Minnesota Press, 1963.

Moul, Keith R. *Theodore Roethke's Career: An Annotated Bibliography*. Boston: G. K. Hall and Company, 1977.

Ostroff, Anthony, ed. *The Contemporary Poet as Artist and Critic*. Boston: Little, Brown & Co., 1964.

Parini, Jay. *Theodore Roethke: An American Romantic*. Amherst, Mass.: University of Massachusetts Press, 1979.

Ross-Bryant, Lynn. *Theodore Roethke: Poetry of the Earth . . . Poet of the Spirit*. Port Washington, N.Y. & London: Kennikat Press, 1981.

Seager, Allan. *The Glass House: The Life of Theodore Roethke*. New York: McGraw-Hill Book Company, 1968.

Schumacher, Paul J. "The Unity of Being: a Study of Theodore Roethke's Poetry." *Ohio University Review*, 12 (1970), 20-40.

Schwartz, Delmore. "The Cunning and the Craft of the Unconscious and Preconscious." *Poetry*, 94 (1959), 203-205.

Slaughter, William R. "Roethke's 'Song.'" *Minnesota Review*, 8 (1968), 342-344.

Spender, Stephen. "Words for the Wind." *New Republic*, 141 (August 10, 1959), 21-22.

Staples, Hugh. "Rose in the Sea-Wind: A Reading of Theodore Roethke's 'North American Sequence.'" *American Literature*, 36 (1964), 189-203.

Stein, Arnold. "Roethke's Memory: Actions, Vision and Revisions." *Northwest Review: Theodore Roethke Special Issue*, 11 (1971), 19-31.

_____, ed. *Theodore Roethke: Essays on the Poetry*. Seattle: University of Washington Press, 1965.

Sullivan, Rosemary. *Theodore Roethke: The Garden Master*. Seattle: The University of Washington Press, 1975.

Williams, Harry. "The Edge Is What I Have": Theodore
    Roethke and After. Lewisburg, Pa.: Bucknell
    University Press, 1977.

Wolff, George. Theodore Roethke. Boston: Twayne
    Publishers, 1981.

                    General References

Aquinas, Thomas. Basic Writings of Saint Thomas
    Aquinas. Ed. and Introd. Anton C. Pegis.
    2 vols. New York: Random House, 1945.

Auden, W. H. "Introduction." The Protestant
    Mystics. Ed. Anne Fremantle. London: Weidenfeld
    and Nicolson, 1964, pp. 3-37.

Bennett, Charles A. A Philosophical Study of
    Mysticism. New Haven: Yale University Press,
    1923.

Berdyaev, Nicolas. Freedom and the Spirit. Trans.
    Oliver Fielding Clarke. 4th ed. London:
    Geoffrey Bles, The Centenary Press, 1948.

_____. The Meaning of the Creative Act. Trans.
    Donald A. Lowrie. New York: The Crowell-Collier
    Publishing Company, 1962.

Blake, William. The Marriage of Heaven and Hell.
    Introd. and Commentary, Sir Geoffrey Keynes.
    London & New York: Oxford University Press, 1975.

_____. Tiriel. Introd. G. E. Bentley, Jr.
    Oxford: Clarendon Press, 1967.

Bodkin, Maud. Archetypal Patterns in Poetry:
    Psychological Studies of Imagination. London:
    Oxford University Press, 1963.

Boehme, Jacob. Six Theosophic Points and Other
    Writings. Trans. John Rolleston Earle. Introd.,
    "Unground and Freedom," Nicolas Berdyaev. Ann
    Arbor: University of Michigan Press, 1970.

Bremond, Abbe Henri. Prayer and Poetry: A
    Contribution to Poetical Theory. Trans. Algar
    Thorold. London: Burns, Oates, and Washbourne,
    1927.

Buber, Martin. I and Thou. Trans. Ronald Gregor
    Smith. 2nd ed. New York: Charles Scribner's
    Sons, 1958.

Bucke, Richard M. Cosmic Consciousness: A Study in
    the Evolution of the Human Mind. New York: E. P.
    Dutton and Company, Inc., 1946.

Buckley, Vincent. Poetry and the Sacred. New York:
    Barnes and Noble, Inc., 1968.

Burke, Kenneth. "Mysticism as a Solution to the Poet's
    Dilemma." Spiritual Problems in Contemporary
    Literature. Ed. Stanley Romain Hopper. New
    York: Harper and Row, 1957.

The Cloud of Unknowing. Edited from the British Museum
    Manuscripts. Introd. Evelyn Underhill. 4th ed.
    London: John M. Watkins, 1946.

Eckhart, Meister. Meister Eckhart: A Modern
    Translation. Ed. and Trans. Raymond Bernard
    Blakney. New York: Harper and Brothers
    Publishers, 1941.

Eliade, Mircea. Patterns in Comparative Religion.
    London: Sheed and Ward, 1958.

Eliot, T. S. Collected Poems 1909-1962. New York:
    Harcourt, Brace and World, Inc., 1970.

Francis de Sales, St. Introduction to the Devout
    Life. Trans. Michael Day. London: Burns and
    Oates, 1956.

Hopkins, Gerard Manley. The Poems of Gerard Manley
    Hopkins. Ed. W.H. Gardner and N.H. MacKenzie.
    4th ed., rev. London: Oxford University Press,
    1970.

Ignatius of Loyola, St. The Text of the Spiritual
    Exercises of Saint Ignatius, Translated from the
    Original Spanish. Pref. John Morris. 4th ed.
    Westminster, Md.: Newman Bookshop, 1943.

Inge, William R. Christian Mysticism. 8th ed.
    London: Methuen and Company, Ltd., 1948.

_____. Mysticism in Religion. Chicago: University
    of Chicago Press, 1948.

James, William. The Varieties of Religious
    Experience: A Study in Human Nature. Ed. and
    Introd. Joseph Ratner. New Hyde Park, New York:
    University Books, 1963.

Jaeger, Werner. The Theology of the Early Greek
    Philosophers. Oxford: The Clarendon Press, 1948.

John of the Cross, St. The Collected Works of St. John
    of the Cross. Trans. Kieran Kavanaugh and Otilio
    Rodriguez. Garden City, New York: Doubleday and
    Company, Inc., 1964.

Johnston, William. The Mysticism of 'The Cloud of
    Unknowing': A Modern Interpretation. Foreward
    Thomas Merton. New York: Desclee Company, 1967.

Kierkegaard, Soren. The Living Thoughts of
    Kierkegaard. Ed. W.H. Auden. Bloomington:
    Indiana University Press, 1966.

Maritain, Jacques. Creative Intuition in Art and
    Poetry. Cleveland and New York: Meridian Books,
    The World Publishing Company, 1966.

Maritain, Jacques and Raissa. The Situation of
    Poetry: Four Essays on the Relations Between
    Poetry, Mysticism, Magic, and Knowledge. New
    York: The Philosophical Library, Inc., 1955.

Martin, F. David. Art and the Religious Experience:
    The 'Language' of the Sacred. Lewisburg, Pa.:
    Bucknell University Press, 1972.

Martz, Louis L. The Poem of the Mind: Essays on
    Poetry, English and American. New York: Oxford
    University Press, 1966.

_____. The Poetry of Meditation: A Study in
    English Religious Literature of the Seventeenth
    Century. rev. ed. New Haven: Yale University
    Press, 1962.

Merton, Thomas. Contemplative Prayer. Garden City,
    N.Y.: Doubleday & Company, Inc., 1971.

Otto, Rudolf. The Idea of the Holy: An Inquiry into
    the Nonrational Factor in the Idea of the Divine
    and its Relation to the Rational. Trans. John W.
    Harvey. 2nd ed. London: Oxford University
    Press, 1970.

_____. Mysticism East and West: A Comparative
Analysis of the Nature of Mysticism. Trans.
Bertha L. Bracey and Richenda C. Payne. New York:
The Macmillan Company, 1932.

Phillips, Robert S. The Confessional Poets.
Carbondale: Southern Illinois University Press,
1973.

Pratt, James B. The Religious Consciousness: A
Psychological Study. New York: The Macmillan
Company, 1921.

Rosenthal, M. L. The New Poets: American and British
Poetry Since World War II. London: Oxford
University Press, 1968.

Rougement, Denis de. Love in the Western World.
Trans. Montgomery Belgion. New York: Harcourt,
Brace and Company, 1940.

Russell, Bertrand. Mysticism and Logic. London:
George Allen & Unwin Ltd., 1917.

Scott, Nathan A. Jr. The Wild Prayer of Longing:
Poetry and the Sacred. New Haven: Yale
University Press, 1971.

Stace, Walter t. Mysticism and Philosophy.
Philadelphia: J. B. Lippincott Company, 1960.

_____, ed. The Teachings of the Mystics. New
York: Mentor, 1960.

Stevens, Wallace. The Palm at the End of the Mind.
Ed. Holly Stevens. New York: Vintage Books,
Random House, 1972.

Suzuki, D. T. Mysticism Christian and Buddhist: The
Eastern and Western Way. New York: Macmillan and
Company, 1969.

Teilhard de Chardin, Pierre. The Phenomenon of Man.
Trans. Bernard Wall. Introd. Sir Julian Huxley.
New York: Harper and Row, Publishers, 1959.

Teresa of Avila, St. The Interior Castle or the
Mansions. Trans. from the Spanish of Saint Teresa
by a Benedictine of Stanbook. Ed. Hugh Martin.
London: SCM Press Ltd., 1958.

Tillich, Paul. The Courage To Be. New Haven: Yale
    University Press, 1971.

_____. The Eternal Now. New York: Charles
    Scribner's Sons, 1963.

Underhill, Evelyn. The Essentials of Mysticism. New
    York: E. P. Dutton & Co., 1920.

_____. Mysticism: A Study in the Nature and
    Development of Man's Spiritual Consciousness.
    12th ed. New York: Meridian Books, 1970.

_____. Practical Mysticism. New York:
    E. P. Dutton & Co., 1919.

Vaughan, Henry. The Complete Poetry of Henry
    Vaughan. Ed. French Fogle. New York: New York
    University Press, 1965.

Watkin, E. I. Poets and Mystics. Freeport, N.Y.:
    Sheed & Ward, Inc., 1953.

Wordsworth, William. The Prelude (1805). Ed. E. de
    Selincourt. London: Oxford University Press,
    1960.

Zaehner, R. C. Mysticism Sacred and Profane: An
    Inquiry into Some Varieties of Praeternatural
    Experience. London: Oxford University Press,
    1973.

INDEX

STUDIES IN ART AND RELIGIOUS INTERPRETATION